SHAPELY ANKLE PREFERR'D

BY THE SAME AUTHOR

The Pineapple
The Woman's Book

SHAPELY ANKLE PREFERR'D

A History of the Lonely Hearts Ad

FRANCESCA BEAUMAN

Chatto & Windus
LONDON

Published by Chatto & Windus 2011

2 4 6 8 10 9 7 5 3 1

First published in Great Britain in 2011 by
Chatto & Windus
Random House, 20 Vauxhall Bridge Road,
London SW1V 2SA
www.rbooks.co.uk

Addresses for companies within The Random House Group Limited can be found at:
www.randomhouse.co.uk/offices.htm

The Random House Group Limited Reg. No. 954009

A CIP catalogue record for this book
is available from the British Library

ISBN 9780701181703

The Random House Group Limited supports The Forest Stewardship
Council (FSC), the leading international forest certification organisation. All our titles
that are printed on Greenpeace approved FSC certified paper carry the FSC logo. Our
paper procurement policy can be found at www.rbooks.co.uk/environment

Mixed Sources
Product group from well-managed
forests and other controlled sources
www.fsc.org Cert no. TT-COC-2139
© 1996 Forest Stewardship Council
FSC

Typeset by Palimpsest Book Production Limited, Falkirk, Stirlingshire
Printed and bound in the UK by
CPI Mackays, Chatham ME5 8TD

Contents

Introduction   vii

Chapter One: *Nine Days Wonder and Laughter*   1

Chapter Two: *A Want of Acquaintance*   13

Chapter Three: *A Feeling Heart*   24

Chapter Four: *Sighs and Lamentations*   47

Chapter Five: *Enterprizing Enamoratos*   69

Chapter Six: *A Private Gentleman*   90

Chapter Seven: *Puffs for Adventurers*   108

Chapter Eight: *The Tomfoolery of Silly Girls*   126

Chapter Nine: *A True Comrade and Friend*   157

Chapter Ten: *Electric Evenings*   181

Notes and Further Reading   195

Index   208

Acknowledgements

Thanks to everyone at Chatto & Windus, especially my editor Jenny Uglow, as well as to my agent Clare Conville and my parents Chris and Nicola Beauman. I am also grateful to David and Susan Bobin and to Jennifer Wilkinson, Jennie Cox and Corinna Csaky for all their support and encouragement. I dedicate this book to my husband, James Bobin, with a thousand thanks and much love.

Introduction

MATRIMONY.——The advertifer is a young Batchelor of 30, of genteel perfon and addrefs, of liberal fentiments, poffeffing an agreeable good temper, and an affable chearful difpofition, would be happy to meet with a young Lady or Widow, poffeffing nearly the fame qualities, who is inclined to enter into that happy ftate, and can command at leaft 5col all above that fum will be fettled upon her for life. As he is a Gentleman of the moft ftrict honour and integrity, the moft profound fecrecy may be relied on, and any Lady may anfwc this without fear or intimidation, and an appointment fhall be returned immediately.——A line addreffed to A. B. at Tom's Coffee-houfe, Cornhill, fhall be punctually attended to.

WEDNESDAY, 4 MARCH 1795. The resignation of the Lord Lieutenant of Ireland was imminent, according to that morning's *Times*. It did not help matters that the Home Secretary was laid up in bed with gout, for it meant he was unable to attend Prime Minister Pitt's Cabinet meetings. All the while, amid blustery spring showers, preparations for the marriage of George, Prince of Wales, to Caroline of Brunswick continued apace.

At least one London gentleman, however, had matters of a more personal nature on his mind. That same morning, an advertisement from 'A.B.' appeared in *The Times*, announcing his search for 'a young Lady or Widow' who would be 'inclined to enter into that happy state' of marriage. Anyone interested was asked to write to him care of Tom's, a coffee-house in the City of London.

This ad is by no means an anomaly. Rather, it is a typical early example of the Lonely Hearts genre, which dates back much further than most people realise and constitutes an enormously rich body of evidence about the qualities that modern Britons have looked for in a husband or wife over the past three centuries. Each of the thousands of ads of this sort that have appeared in newspapers, magazines and pamphlets offers a glimpse through a window into the life of one ordinary person, a person who in all likelihood had never seen himself or herself in print before and whose voice we rarely hear. These tiny pockets of text are like those double minia-ture portraits that were once so popular: one side contains a self-portrait, but the other side has yet to be filled in. That is the job of the reader.

Most of those who have placed Lonely Hearts ads over the years have done so with a view to marriage. The only human society that has *not* made marriage in one form or another central to the way it is organised is the Na people, of which there are about 30,000 living in the Yunnan Province of southwest China. They live in sibling-based households, and sexual relations occur in the form of *nan-sese*, meaning 'to visit furtively': the men walk to the houses of the women at night, but return in the morning. They are, however, the sole exception in recorded history. In western Europe making a 'good' marriage, or for that matter any marriage at all, was for a long time the ultimate goal, especially for women. In a society based around the rituals of the Christian Church, it was the only context in which sexual relations were sanctioned. It was also a matter of economic prudence, both for the upper classes who had property to protect and for the working classes who sought to share life's practical burdens. Marriage was a social, economic and political necessity, the foundation upon which polite (and not-so-polite) society was built.

These days, the media is full of the trials and tribulations of those having trouble tracking down Mr or Ms 'Right', or even Mr or Ms 'They'll Do'. But those of us who despair of finding someone

to walk down the aisle with might spare a thought for our predecessors 100, 200 or 300 years ago who faced the same predicament.
It is, after all, almost entirely a matter of luck. There are some who
will bossily counsel you to visualise a mate, or get a new haircut,
or never call the other person back, or learn to love yourself. Rubbish.
There is no secret trick. As the hero of *Lady Audley's Secret* (1862), by
Mary Braddon, muses:

> As if happiness were not essentially accidental – a bright and
> wandering bird, utterly irregular in its migration; with us one
> summer's day, and for ever gone from us the next! Look at
> matrimony, for instance . . . Who is to say which shall be the
> one judicious selection out of the nine hundred and ninety-
> nine mistakes? Who shall decide from the first aspect of the
> slimy creature, which is to be the one eel out of the colossal
> bag of snakes?

There are, however, actions one can take to maximise one's luck,
and these include placing – or replying to – a Lonely Hearts ad.

Chapter One

Nine Days Wonder and Laughter

THE GOLDEN FLEECE pub in the heart of the City of London was an unlikely place for romance to blossom. Standing on the corner of Gracechurch Street and Eastcheap Street, it was a dirty, smoky, disreputable establishment, the scene of fist-fights more often than love trysts. Yet it was here, on 19 July 1695, that the world's first Lonely Hearts ad (at least, the first of which there is still evidence) was published. On page three of one of the many weekly pamphlets for sale on the streets of the capital, surrounded by advertisements for a cobbler's apprentice, an Arabian stallion and a second-hand bed, was this brave plea:

> A Gentleman about 30 Years of Age, that says he had a Very Good Estate, would willingly Match himself to some Good Young Gentlewoman that has a Fortune of 3000l. or thereabouts, and he will make Settlement to Content.

A few lines further down, a second bachelor in search of a wife revealed himself:

> A Young Man about 25 Years of Age, in a very good Trade, and whose Father will make him worth 1000l. would willingly embrace a suitable Match. He has been brought up a Dissenter, with his Parents, and is a sober Man.

Brief and to the point as these ads were, they were still enough to cause the streets of London to echo with excited chatter all the way through the long, hot, smelly summer months.

Who *were* these young men? It is possible to catch a glimpse of them at least. The first offers the rather vague boast that he has 'a Very Good Estate', and is aged about thirty. Since the average age at which men got married in this period was twenty-seven and a half, he was just at the stage when his parents would be beginning to pester him about settling down. His criteria in a prospective wife are that she should be 'good', 'young' and rich. The second advertiser has been raised as a Dissenter (that is, Protestant, but outside the Church of England), and a sober one at that. He also claims that he is due to inherit the by-no-means-shabby sum of £1,000, the equivalent of about £100,000 in today's money.

These ads encapsulate a central tenet of human mate choice: men want a partner who is young. Next most important on the list are looks, domestic prowess and resources, or 'Comeliness, Prudence and 5 or 600l. in Money, Land or Joynture . . .' as an ad in the same publication the following month phrased it. These criteria occur again and again, not only throughout the history of Lonely Hearts ads, but throughout the history of human courtship generally, according to contemporary studies of the subject.

Many no doubt bought a copy of the pamphlet solely for the voyeuristic pleasure of trying to work out the identity of the would-be suitors. Was it a friend? A neighbour? Were they in earnest? While some might have pretended to be shocked by the innovation, others probably secretly thought that advertising for a wife was rather a clever idea. The publisher of the pamphlet in which the ads appeared, *A Collection for Improvement of Husbandry and Trade*, was a popular local figure named John Houghton. After graduating from Cambridge, Houghton had set himself up as an apothecary and also as dealer in tea, coffee and chocolate. He is better remembered, however, for being one of the first people to appreciate the possibilities of the advertising game, and hence the first to make proper money out of it. The pages of his *Collection* advertised all kinds of merchandise; so why not men and women? It was not really such a leap. With all the ads composed in the third person, Houghton, as editor, ensured that he positioned himself as the instigator. Furthermore, following the lapsing of the Licensing Act eight weeks earlier, which in effect established a free press, he no longer had the censor to fear in his decisions over what to print.

By commercialising matchmaking, Houghton brought marriage into line with situations vacant, rooms to rent, the arrival of a consignment of tea from the Indies – it was the provision of just another service that urban dwellers (and Londoners especially) needed. Even so, in a note next to the Lonely Hearts ads, he felt the need to assert that they were 'honourable' in every respect, as well as to reassure potential suitors that 'no body shall know any thing of the matter, but where I shall reasonably believe they are in good earnest'. So unconventional was this method of finding a mate that the stigma that accompanied it was inevitable, and secrecy a top priority. It was the price Houghton paid for publicly positioning himself as the creator of the Lonely Hearts industry.

Houghton was keenly aware of the ads' novelty value: 'When it shall appear that I am Candid, and no[t] otherwise concerned than in bringing two Elderly Persons to a Treaty; and the Nine Days Wonder and Laughter (usually attending new things) are over . . . then 'tis probable such Advertisements may prove useful.' From the start, then, Lonely Hearts ads were a source of entertainment, with many reading them simply to laugh at them. Indeed, the hope that they might boost sales was probably one reason for publishing them in the first place, and the reason they were set in a much larger, bolder font than the other 'Accounts of News from the little World' that surrounded them. Houghton, a shrewd businessman, doubtless had an instinct that they were a sure-fire way to attract readers; he may even have made up the ads himself with this very aim in mind, even though the following fortnight, when the ads appeared once more, he rebuffed the suggestion – 'These Proposals for Matches are real,' he protested.

By April of the following year, 1696, Houghton's venture had become such a success that he was able to claim: '[t]heir own Parents shall not manage it more to their Satisfaction, and the more comes to me the better, I shall be able to serve them.' Clearly, there was a demand for the service he provided – anything, surely, to ease the agony of the courtship process.

Among the upper echelons of society, a tight-knit network of family, friends and neighbours was crucial to success in the marriage market, as were parties or church services, which were among the select occasions where genteel young men and women were allowed – and even encouraged – to mingle. Lower down the social scale there was the workplace. In rural areas, hiring fairs were a popular place to meet, as were alehouses and market-places. Local celebrations throughout the year also provided regular opportunities for the young people of the village to bat their eyelashes at each other: Shrove Tuesday, May Day, harvest festivals in the summer and Christmas in the winter. Life happened primarily outdoors and in a very public fashion, and hence courtship did too – you met in public, courted in public, kissed in public. Particularly during the early stages of courtship, the young tended to be left to their own devices. Outside the upper gentry and aristocracy, the sexes were almost entirely free to mingle, even to be alone together. While official marriage brokers were rare, there were plenty of unofficial matchmakers (neighbours, great-aunts, employers) eager to help. Parents were also involved, of course, though less so than is often assumed; the initiative generally lay with the young person, and arranged marriages were almost unheard of outside the aristocracy (and even there they were not common).

Frontispiece to a popular seventeenth-century courtship manual, *The Misteries of Love and Eloquence, Or the Arts of Wooing and Complementing* by Edward Phillips (1658)

What was arguably the world's first Agony Column, the *Athenian Mercury*, was founded in 1691, three years into the reign of William and Mary. The paper gives a vivid sense of the difficulties involved when parents attempted to influence their children's choice of partner. In one instance, 'A Gentlewoman about Eighteen Years of Age, and a tolerable Fortune, is Courted by a Person of Fifty eight, who is very well received by her Parents . . .' The 'Gentlewoman' in question, however, 'could not her self for some time be prevailed with, at which her Parents were not a little displeased, but she being of a good Disposition, and her Relations using some Arguments with her, as the great Scarcity of good Husbands in these days, and the Hopes of a good Estate, seems to have wrought upon her . . .'

And so, in response to the question 'How far the Duty of a Child does oblige her to comply with her Parents . . . ?', the *Athenian Mercury* advised that 'She must not obstinately refuse the Advice of her Parents, tho' on the other side they have no Power to force her contrary to her Inclinations.' In other words, it was fair to expect a bit of give and take. High mortality rates meant that many young people had already lost one or both parents by the time they reached marriageable age, with the result that they were essentially free to marry whomever they chose. For women, there was the additional fear of 'the great Scarcity of good Husbands in these days', a fear that seems to have afflicted almost every generation in some way.

The 1690s were a transformative decade for the institution of marriage. Having a married couple on the English throne meant that heterosexual monogamy was now more than ever perceived as the 'normal' mode of living. Furthermore, William and Mary had not inherited the throne in the way their predecessors had, but rather had been contracted to it by a Whig government anxious for change. John Locke argued in his *Two Treatises of Government* (1689) that this shift in the source of social, political and moral authority would and should have significant implications for the future of the family too: the dominant patriarchal relationship would and should no longer be inherited (that is, with one's father) but should instead be contracted 'between two free, equal, consenting adults'. Thus Locke advocated a distinctly more modern interpretation of marriage, with the result that the issue of marriage in general became very much part of the public discourse, whether on Fleet Street or Drury Lane. The plot of the Restoration play *Love for Love* by William Congreve (1695), for instance, centres upon a tyrannical parent, Sir Sampson, who tries to arrange his son Valentine's marriage purely for financial gain, but whose authority is challenged ('mayn't I do what I please?' asks Valentine) by a more consultative approach to the matter.

At the same time, the rise of economic individualism, where the husband *and* the wife both earned their own wage rather than just contributing to the family kitty, meant that this was a period of significant change for the family. The patriarchal family unit, where everyone lived together (grandparents, cousins, servants) was gradually being replaced by the conjugal family unit, or what we would nowadays call the nuclear family. This made one's choice of a partner more important than ever before. It determined not only who one lived with, but also one's social and economic circumstances: it was just you, your husband or wife and your children staring at each other across the breakfast table, for ever and ever until death did you part.

In London, however, tracking down a husband or wife was not always easy. About 8,000 rural migrants arrived in the city every year in search of work, wages and in many cases a wife, as a consequence of which by 1690 the population topped half a million. New survival strategies were required to keep one's head above water in this huge, frantic, anonymous pool of people. In particular, it was no longer possible for tradesmen to rely upon word-of-mouth to publicise products and share information – hence the rise of advertising.

The first advertisement to appear in an English newspaper was published in 1625. It informed Londoners of the publication of a pamphlet about the marriage of the Prince of Wales to Henrietta

Maria, the daughter of the late King of France. Ads of a more personal nature were soon a regular feature of newspapers and periodicals – horses for sale, houses for rent, servants wanted – and before long became subject to parody. On the same day (16 May 1660) that Charles II, while in The Hague, received a delegation from both Houses of Parliament asking him to return to England as King, an obscure London periodical known as *Mercurius Fumigosus* offered up an ad purporting to be from a 'worthy, plump, fresh, free and willing Widdow liveth near the Carpenrer in Flowre and Dean street near Spittle-fields' who was in search of 'any man that is Able to labour in her Corporation'. 'If any man want a wife and come to this pure piece of iniquity,' the ad went on, 'let him present the true picture of his Tool there's no question but he may find favour . . .' Whether it was also a parody of some very early Lonely Hearts ads that have since been lost to us is impossible to know. What is not in doubt, however, is that it was a response to decades of Puritan repression. Austere prudishness was out; sexual innuendo was in. The nation was eager for a little light relief, which *Mercurius Fumigosus* was pleased to provide. There was much bawdy humour to be had, after all, in aligning a sexually voracious widow with all the other commodities on offer in the pages of the London press.

A worthy plump, freſh, free and willing Widdow liveth near the Carpenrer in Flowre and Dean ſtreet near Spittle-fields, ſhe is in great diſtreſſe for want of a Lancktaradiddledino, and would accept of any man that is Able to labour in her Corporation, but in the firſt place ſhe deſires to make tryal of *A B E L* nigh Roſemary Lane who is now turn'd Witch, and tels fortunes, and craveth the aſſiſtance of her Brother a pretended Aſs-trologer, who when he wants 'mployment, handles his ſhettle and Loom to repleniſh his hungry Maw. If any man want a wife and come to this pure piece of iniquity, let him preſent the true picture of his Tool there's no queſtion but he may find favour, and commit Poultry without Matrimony.

Mercurius Fumigosus, 16 May 1660

A few weeks later, the small ads were afforded a royal seal of approval when the King himself placed a 'Lost' ad in *Mercurius Publicus* for 'a smooth black dog, less than a grey-hound', which, if found, should be returned to 'His Majesties Back Stairs'. After a further few days the request was repeated, but this time in a rather more desperate tone:

> We must call upon you again for a Black Dog between the greyhound and a spaniel, no white about him only a streak on his breast, and tayl a little bobbed. It is His Majesties own dog, and doubtless was stolen. Whoever finds him may acquaint any at Whitehall for the dog was better known at Court than those who stole him. Will they never leave robbing His Majestie? Must he not keep a dog?

One might have thought Charles II would have had more pressing matters to attend to: he had been back in London and on the throne for less than a month when he placed the ad. On the other hand, perhaps this was precisely why he missed his trusty canine companion so much.

The reign of Charles II proved to be a significant moral departure from England's Puritan past, and this was reflected in the rise of humorous journals such as *Poor Robin's Intelligence*, which focused exclusively on matters of marriage and sex ('Poor Robin' was slang for penis). A typical entry is a newsflash about an outbreak of horn plague in Cuckoldshire and, short-lived as the journal was (it lasted only eighteen months), it is a fascinating reflection of the state of sexual politics in London at the time, in particular because it was aimed at the city's increasingly literate shopkeepers and tradesmen. In 1676, it featured an ad from a 'Worcestershire Gentlewoman' with £300 a year and a 'face just of the complexion of a Garden-walk new gravel'd', who wanted to marry 'any thriving Gentleman, professing the Ingenious mystery of Chimney-scouring'. The joke was that the reason she needed to resort to an ad to find a husband was that she was so extraordinarily ugly that otherwise there was no way any man would agree to the arrangement, despite the lure of money. It also mocked the essentially practical basis of many marriages. In doing so, however, it helped establish the linguistic conventions of the genuine Lonely Hearts ads that were to appear in Houghton's *Collection* some years later.

A *Worcestershire* Gentlewoman, born under the malevolent aspect of a Tar e-penny Planet, but by continual industry over-ruling her stars arrived to the vast fortune of three hundred pound, *per annum*, during the date of Elbow-grease ; whose person without Pattins is much about the height of a short Long-Lane-petticoat , and her face just of the complexion of a Garden-walk new gravel'd, is desirous to enter into the honourable state of Matrimony ; if any thriving Gentleman, professing the Ingenious mystery of Chimney-scowring, have a mind to so considerable a fortune, let him speedily enter his name at the Match-Brokers office, and he shall be further satisfied.

Poor Robin's Intelligence, 17 October 1676

Poor Robin's Intelligence also pioneered another notable new form of text, the satirical catalogue that advertised husbands and wives for sale. These were at their most popular in 1691; in that year *Mercurius Matrimonialis*, for example, featured ads for 'A lusty, stout proportion'd Man, had a good estate before the Fire [of London], and is still fit for Womans Service' and 'A Commission Officer, full of Courage, brim full of Honour, a well proportion'd Man, and very beautiful, and yet wants Money'. In a similar pamphlet in August, women supposedly for sale included 'A tobacconist's daughter in Watling Street, very pretty but wild. If taken with all her faults her father gives £400'; 'A quack's widow in Thames Street, worth when all legacies paid, besides a vast stock of pills and elixirs, £1000'; and 'A coffeeman's daughter about the Temple. Her only fault she squints a little. £100.' These women are uniformly described in relation to the men who controlled them; they are always somebody's daughter, somebody's wife or somebody's widow. They could be viewed in Lincoln's Inn Gardens between 5 p.m. and 9 p.m. that Sunday: 'All gentleman will be accepted who have clear limbs and members entire upon examination.' It is easy to picture a group of friends sitting around in a coffee-house composing the catalogues, coming up with ever more outrageous descriptions, laughing raucously as they did so, wine goblet in hand. Yet so convincing were these catalogues that a flurry of letters appeared in the London press demanding to know whether or not they were genuine.

A society jokes about whatever makes it anxious, and in England in the 1690s it was the state of the marriage market. Even the theatres of Drury Lane were dominated by the topic. Joining Congreve's *Love for Love* (1695) were *The Old Bachelor* (1693) and *The Mourning Bride* (1697), as well as *The Provoked Wife* (1697) by John Vanbrugh and *Love and a Bottle* (1698) by George Farquhar. The titles alone make it clear that the central themes were consistently love and marriage, and peopling these productions were the stock characters of late Restoration comedy – wealthy widows, innocent maidens, cuckolded husbands – who also featured in the various other forms of contemporary literature that poked fun at the subject. Taken together, they offer a fundamentally cynical examination of the follies and foibles of late Restoration society.

It is not impossible that it was as a result of going to the theatre, browsing the latest journals or flicking through a just-published catalogue that John Houghton conceived the idea of using his *Collection* to offer some genuine assistance to those who found themselves floundering in the quagmire of the late seventeenth-century marriage market. With William and Mary firmly in power, England was experiencing a measure of political stability for the first time in many years. Urban culture was also increasingly dominant; the establishment of the Bank of England in 1694, which resulted in the rise of the City of London as a social and economic force, further accelerated the pace of change, not only in the capital, but across the nation. The 1690s were arguably the first decade of what we now call modern Britain, and the appearance of the first Lonely Hearts ads was one manifestation of this.

Chapter Two

A Want of Acquaintance

A gentleman who, on the twentieth instant, had the honour to conduct a lady out of a boat at Whitehall Stairs, desires to know where he may wait on her to disclose a matter of concern. A letter directed to Mr Samuel Reeves, to be left with Mr May, at the Golden Head, the upper end of New Southampton Street, Covent Garden.

BRITAIN'S FIRST 'ONCE Seen' ad, as they are now known, appeared in *The Tatler* in 1709, the year the magazine was founded. Such ads played a vital role in a world before telephones or even telegrams, when a brief glimpse of a pretty face across a busy street might be all one got before she disappeared into the crowd. In the above instance it is one Samuel Reeves who regrets the missed opportunity. There is no way of knowing, of course, whether this was his real name. Records show that there was a Samuel Reeves who was born in Derby in 1689. His mother Susannah died when he was just eleven, so perhaps it was then that he travelled south. By 1709 he would have been twenty, and just beginning to think seriously about his marriage prospects. Indeed, he might even be the same Samuel Reeves who married in Hexham in Northumberland in 1710. One can only speculate.

Neither 'Once Seen' ads nor more conventional Lonely Hearts ads were by any means common yet, but they did exist; you just had to know where to look. *The Tatler* was one of an unprecedented number of magazines and newspapers founded in the late seventeenth and early eighteenth centuries. Within four days of the lapsing of the Licensing Act in 1695, the newspaper the *Flying Post* hit the streets of London, followed a month later by the *Post Boy*, as well as Houghton's *Collection* and many others. The nation's first successful daily newspaper, the *Daily Courant*, was established in 1702, and it was swiftly followed by a flurry of others. With the press no longer forced to operate underground, a cacophony of new voices emerged. Such democratisation meant that it was possible for almost anyone and everyone with means to see themselves in print, whether in the news section, on the letters page or even in Monday morning's personal column. (It has always been the case that most ads are placed over the weekend, the result presumably of a long, lonely weekend spent in the company of just a dog and a bottle of cheap red wine.)

By 1710 England boasted fifty-three newspapers, with a total circulation of approximately two million, and all carried ads of one sort or another. The voyeuristic pleasure they gave was highlighted by Joseph Addison in an essay he wrote that year for *The Tatler*: 'I must confess, I have a certain Weakness in my Temper, that is often very much affected by these little Domestick Occurences, and have frequently been caught with Tears in my Eyes over a melancholy Advertisement.' A couple of weeks later, a letter appeared in the magazine offering assistance to those seeking to place a Lonely Hearts ad. It included a sample ad written for a friend, featuring a thirty-year-old gentleman 'with dark-coloured Hair, bright Eye, and a long Nose' who was rich enough to offer his prospective bride 'a Coach and Horses, and a proportionable Settlement' and was in search of 'a good-humoured, tall, fair, young Woman, of about 3000l. Fortune'. In other words, here was a dark, handsome, wealthy man in search of a young, blonde, wealthy woman — a standard trope that would manifest itself again and again.

In 1712 the nascent newspaper trade was nearly destroyed by the Stamp Act, which placed a tax of one shilling on every ad accepted for publication. This difficulty was overcome, however, by the likes of the *Daily Advertiser*, the *Public Advertiser* and the *General Advertiser*, which from the beginning consisted entirely of ads. The intention was that it would be these 'pieces of *domestic* intelligence' themselves that would lure readers, which indeed they did, being 'much more interesting than those paragraphs which our daily historians generally give us, under the title of home news . . . the ads are filled with matters of great importance, both to the great, vulgar and the small.' This did not go unnoticed by the conventional press, where the classifieds almost always appeared on the front page. The result was that a web of interconnected stories stared out at the reader; it was the story of a metropolis, related in forty-word bursts. This was noted by, among others, Samuel Johnson, who found that, when reading the news, '. . . his attention is diverted to other thoughts, by finding that Mirza will not cover this season, or that a spaniel has been lost or stolen, that answers to the name of Roger'.

'Promise, large promise, is the soul of an advertisement,' Johnson went on, and most of those who advertised in this period were clearly in accord. The majority were in their mid-twenties, all mentioned money and all were men; 'an agreeable young gentleman in trade' was a typical description. Others were more loquacious, like the 'Native of North Britain, (but with very little of the Brogue) of a genteel Profession, tall in Stature, finely shaped and well proportioned, has a delicate Head of Hair, white Hand, a large Calf, strong Back, broad Shoulders, and is what the World generally terms of a good-natured Disposition', who sought 'an agreeable young Lady, not exceeding Thirty-four, of some Fortune, who has no Objection to the Scotch Method of Courtship'. It was also common to trumpet one's health: this was an era in which many died young, and what was the point in going through the whole rigmarole of a wedding only to have one's other half pop their clogs on the first night of the honeymoon? It was perhaps this very night that the 'gentleman of 2000l. a year, fifty two years of age next July, but of a vigorous, strong, and amorous consti-tution' alluded to in his ad in the *Daily Advertiser* in 1750.

The Lonely Hearts ad was an entirely new form of text to emerge in this period. Not only did it differ from conventional forms of textual courtship, such as love poetry, in that it tended to be the man's virtues that were the focus, rather than the woman's, but it was also a new paradigm for fiction. Rich? Handsome? Thirty-some-thing? Don't believe a word of it. Lonely Hearts ads have always been laced with lies and white lies and half-truths. The art of adver-tising is, by its nature, about creating a fantasy world: life as we want it to be, rather than as it really is.

Lonely Hearts ads established themselves in the mainstream press just as the first novels appeared in bookshops, and the two share a number of characteristics. *Robinson Crusoe* (1719) by Daniel Defoe, *Pamela* (1740) by Samuel Richardson and *Joseph Andrews* (1742) by Henry Fielding all demonstrate a new-found focus on the indi-vidual. Following a mini-sketch of the title character, the reader is then allowed to peer into their private lives to find out what it is they want, need, crave. And these novels, again like Lonely Hearts ads, provided communities with a shared interest to discuss over the garden fence or in the coffee-house: 'Have you reached the brilliant bit in Chapter Six yet where . . . ?' 'Did you see that ad in the *Gazetteer* today?'

The novels may even have influenced contemporary perceptions of what constituted the ideal woman. In the preface to *Clarissa* (1747–8), Richardson lauds the 'delicacy of sentiments, particularly with regard to the other sex' that his title character demonstrates; and, indeed, 'delicacy' is a quality that recurs with increasing frequency in Lonely Hearts ads of the period. For example, a gentleman in the *Daily Advertiser* in 1750 hoped for a wife with:

good teeth, soft lips, sweet breath, with eyes no matter what colour, so they are but expressive; of a healthy complexion, rather inclin'd to fair than brown; neat in her person, her bosom full, plump, firm and white; a good understanding, without being a wit, but cheerful and lively in conversation, polite and delicate of speech, her temper humane and tender, and to look as if she could feel delight where she wishes to give it.

Should such a perfect specimen exist, she was asked to write to 'A.B.' at the Smyrna, a popular coffee-house on the north side of Pall Mall (which, a few years later, achieved notoriety for having regularly hosted the French spy Florence Hensey. Clearly there were all sorts of intrigues going on there other than just drinking coffee).

There were some men, though, for whom money eclipsed all else. They were clear that marriage was a business transaction:

> ... if any Widow having no Children, and keeps a Grocer's Shop, is inclinable to alter her Condition in the Way of Marriage, to a Widower of the same Business (and one of considerable Fortune) is desired to direct to Mrs Susan Palmer, living in Cage-Lane, Stroud, Rochester, where they may hear further ...

(Mrs Palmer was presumably a respectable local, older woman who lived nearby, for it was common to channel Lonely Hearts enquiries through her kind.)

There were some ads – such as the one that appeared in a London newspaper in 1756 from 'A Gentleman of twenty-five Years of Age [who] has a great Dependence upon the Death of a Relation that is not young', who sought a woman with £60–70 a year who was 'agreeable', under thirty and, ideally, spoke another language – that made it clear there were money troubles to be dealt with. As a result, it was common to mention the marriage contract early on: something along the lines of 'would make a handsome Settlement according to her Fortune' was standard.

Some sought to explain why they had decided to approach the courtship process in such an unconventional fashion. '[T]he real Foundation of applying in this public Way, is a Want of Acquaintance in London sufficient to introduce me in a private one,' lamented one lonely gentlemen in 1750. Others imagined that an ad might help them find a wife in a hurry, like the forty-year-old with £600 a year who 'is inclinable to marry, (but not willing to have a long Courtship)'. Sometimes the impetus to marry was more practical: in a rare example in this period of a Lonely Hearts ad outside London, in 1746 a 'Bachelor not above 60 with a clear Estate of 5000l. per Annum' advertised in the *Cambridge Journal*, which had been founded two years earlier, for a woman who could provide him with an heir. Not surprisingly, this caused quite a kerfuffle in the area, with one wag writing in to the newspaper to let the advertiser know that she could provide him with an heir in just four months if he was really that desperate.

But were any of these ads successful? If they were, the participants would have kept it secret, and hence no records survive. It is only occasionally that one is allowed a glimpse of what happened next. 'A young man wants a wife with two or three hundred pounds; or the money will do without the wife: – whoever will advance it shall have five per Cent' was an ad that appeared in the *Daily Advertiser* in 1759. It piqued the 'unconquerable curiosity' of one woman who (as she explained on the letters page of the *Lady's Magazine* later that year) felt able to reply only because she saw no risk to her reputation: 'My years protected me, for I own more than forty,' the implication being that no man would seek to take advantage of someone so incredibly *old*. It turned out that the ad had been placed by a young German man by the name of Gerand, 'his dress and aspect plain; his countenance honest: a ruddy circle bloomed upon his cheeks; and his eyes spoke plain integrity'. They arranged to meet, and it transpired that he wanted the money in order to establish himself in trade, though what sort of trade he did not mind. After some discussion, the woman agreed to invest in him (it was purely a business arrangement, though, with no mention of marriage) and a few weeks later the doors opened on Gerand's, a high-class haberdashery shop on the Strand.

'The Taste of the Times is wholly turned to Joking,' wrote Lady Mary Wortley Montagu, and indeed by 1740 Lonely Hearts ads had become a common enough feature of London life to be satirised in the *Gentleman's Magazine*, now in its ninth year of existence. A letter appeared allegedly from a sixty-three-year-old bachelor, 'Somewhat infirm'd of Body, but perfectly Sound of Mind', by the name of Solomon Single. 'Sir, I am very bashful' was how he explained his need to advertise, continuing that 'I know if I have a very fine, beautiful, accomplish'd young Lady, (and such a one only will I have) my Money must buy her; therefore I endeavour to get such a Purchase with as little Trouble as possible, and that is my Occasion of writing this Letter to you.' In this way, the piece highlighted the increasingly commercial nature of the courtship process.

The next issue of the magazine printed a selection of supposed replies to the oh-so-romantic Mr Single's plea. Every archetype of mid-eighteenth-century womanhood is represented: an actress named Lucy Flirt, a chambermaid seeking to elude engagement to the local chaplain, a Herefordshire lady who boasts of her ability to 'make Jellies, and Soups', another who the morning before had read in her coffee granules that a husband would soon present himself, and finally Rachel Downright, who told it like it was: 'Thou art an old Fool. Grow wiser, and die a Batchelor.'

Another ad of 1740, however, was a little less transparent about the fact that it was undoubtedly inserted in jest.

If any Lady, not yet past her grand Climacterick, of a comfort-
able Fortune in her own Disposal, is desirous of spending the
Remainder of her Life with a tolerably handsome young Fellow,
of great Parts, about five Feet six Inches, may hear of such a
one to her Mind, by enquiring at the Theatre Coffee-House
for Mr F, a Sophister of —— College Cambridge.
        Note. He is short-sighted.

Here is one of the first instances of the soon oft-repeated joke that
the advertiser was 'short-sighted', in other words, that the ad was
designed to appeal solely to the ugly – who on earth else would
turn to the personal columns to find a husband?

Yet it remains impossible to know whether the advertiser who,
in 1750, claimed that such ads 'are often inserted by Gentleman
for their Diversion' was accurate in his assessment. Certainly, this
was the perception (fraud, quackery and scams like the South Sea
Bubble fiasco were a feature of the age), which is why many advertisers sought to reassure potential respondents that 'She may
depend on all the Behaviour that can be expected from a Man
of Honour, however the Event of such Meeting may prove . . . I
do therefore declare myself in earnest.' It was worth emphasising,
for the description 'a Man of Honour' was certainly not one that
could be applied to all those who placed ads. Take the 'single
gentleman of character and fortune' who the same year placed an
appeal in the *Daily Advertiser* for a woman who was willing to live
with him 'first as an house-keeper, afterwards, if lik'd, as a
companion for life'.

In the years since *The Tatler* had first introduced 'Once Seen'
ads to the nation, they too had flourished, largely in response to
the huge growth in the number of publications keen to carry
them. In 1748 the *General Advertiser* printed a plea to 'a lady, genteelly
dressed, [who] was seen to lead a string of beautiful stone-horses

through Edmonton, Tottenham, and Newington', from a gentleman 'smitten with her behavior'. He proposed a deal: if, on meeting, she decided she did not want to marry him, he would buy all her horses from her instead. Ten years later, an appeal appeared in the *London Chronicle* for 'A Young Lady who was at Vauxhall on Thursday night last, in company with two Gentlemen', who had been spotted by:

> a young Gentleman in blue and a gold-laced hat, who, being near her by the Orchestra during the performance, especially the last song, gazed upon her with the utmost attention . . . He earnestly hopes (if unmarried) she will favour him with a line directed to A.D. at the bar of the Temple Exchange Coffee-house, Temple-bar, to inform him whether Fortune, Family, and Character, may not entitle him, upon a further knowl-edge, to hope an interest in her Heart.

It often seems to be the case that women are most attractive to men when they are with other men.

An anthology of these ads published in 1750 also suggests that they were one of the few literary contexts of the period in which women's voices were heard, among them a cry for the 'young Gent who appeared last Monday at the Ball at Vintners Hall, dress'd in a French-grey Frock, laced with Silker, a plain yellow Sattin Waistcoat, white Stockings, and a plain Hat', who had 'greatly enamour'd a Lady then present', which was placed in the paper by 'the Lady's Friends'. The website *www.mysinglefriend.com* may be a brilliant idea, but it is by no means a new one.

By 1760 London was the home to four daily newspapers and five tri-weekly newspapers, while those in the provinces numbered more than thirty-five; the rapid expansion of the press meant that there was no shortage of places to insert 'Once Seen' ads. In London at least, with its rapidly increasing population, there was a signif-

icant need for this sort of service. As the newspaper proprietor
Nathaniel Mist put it, 'it is certain that in a great and populous
City like this, where the Inhabitants of one End of the Town are
Strangers to the Trade and Way of Living of those of the other,
many Things which prove to be of singular Use and Benefit could
never be known to the World by any other Means but this of
advertising . . .' From the 'Gentleman in a Spencer Wig . . . at the

The Laughing Audience by William Hogarth (1733). The theatre was a
frequent site of romantic intrigue.

Lord Mayor's Ball' to the 'lady who had on a pink coloured capuchin, edged with ermine . . . at Drury Lane Playhouse', not only do 'Once Seen' ads offer up a potted history of fashion in their detailed descriptions of what the mysterious person wore, but they also give a wonderfully vivid sense of what London was like in the first half of the eighteenth century: everyone toing and froing, bustling around, off to a ball or to the theatre. Catch her eye through a crowd, try frantically to weave one's way across a cobbled street, dodging the horses and carriages and manure, but just at that moment – oh no! – with a twitch of her dress and a flash of her bonnet, she's gone. For ever? Let's hope not.

Chapter Three

A Feeling Heart

ATE ONE AFTERNOON in 1776, a carriage clattered to a halt outside the Cocoa Tree Coffee House on Pall Mall. The side door swung open, and on to the muddy cobbles stepped a gentleman who was strangely muffled up, considering that the weather was relatively warm for that time of year. He glanced one way down the street, then the other, and strode determinedly through the Cocoa Tree's front entrance, his manservant scuttling behind him. It was time for him to collect the replies to a Lonely Hearts ad he had placed in a London daily newspaper a few days prior. 'M.L.' described himself as a 'Gentleman of genteel Address, and easy circumstances, who has tasted sufficiently of life, to be thoroughly convinced that real enjoyment consists alone in domestic retirements, could be happy to renounce that phantom, which the generality of mankind pursues under the idea of pleasure'. He was after a woman of 'genteel education, and possessed of accomplishments sufficient to adorn a middle sphere of life'. Today's visit to the Cocoa Tree was one of considerable import. Would the woman of his dreams reveal herself to him? Or, indeed, any woman at all?

Inside, the Cocoa Tree bustled with activity. It was a well-respected club frequented predominantly by government figures and civil servants; perhaps M.L. was one of their number. Some were there to discuss the recent fighting in the American colonies, others to read the papers in peace and – unlikely as it might seem – one or perhaps two were there to find a wife.

The Coffee House by H. Bunbury, engraved by W. Dickinson (1794). Were one or two of these gentlemen secretly in search of a wife?

M.L. approached the bar and asked the barmaid – one of the few women present – whether there was any post for him. With a knowing wink, she slid a pile of letters across the shiny bar. M.L.'s heart skipped a beat. He even felt a little faint; the suspense was just too much. 'Come hither you,' M.L. said to his manservant (or, at least, this is how the Irish playwright Isaac Bickerstaffe dramatised such a moment in his 1767 play, *Love in the City*):

hold this parcel of letters for me – it is what my advertisement brought me in three hours – Let me see – here is one sealed with a thimble – That should be from some superannuated temptress; at all events, I will put it into the left hand pocket – Two doves billing – that should be something pretty – I am a gentlewoman come to misfortunes, if I had any thing to say to you – in with the other – Here's one seal'd with the pipe of a key; another with a piece of smoaky sealing-wax, and a wet thumb . . .

M.L. claimed in his ad that, 'Fortune is by no means an inducement to the Advertiser'. Assuming this statement is to be taken at face value, it reflects an important shift in priorities in the search for wedded bliss. Decreasing emphasis was being placed on economic considerations; instead, romantic love had, for many, become the most important factor. Academics have long debated the extent to which marriage evolved in the eighteenth century, but recent scholarship has concluded that 'By the end of the 1700s personal choice of partners had replaced arranged marriage as a social ideal, and individuals were encouraged to marry for love. For the first time in five thousand years, marriage came to be seen as a private relationship between two individuals rather than one link in a larger system of political and economic alliances.' Underscored by Enlightenment thinking, which promoted the pursuit of happiness as a valid goal, many men increasingly sought a wife whose primary role was to be not (just) an economic asset, but someone with whom they could genuinely share and enjoy their life.

In 1769, one would-be suitor pondered the qualities he hoped for in a wife: 'good-tempered, sensible, and can sit by a genteel fire-side, and converse with gentlemen of understanding and liberal education'. His vision of married life – sitting by a warm hearth while his wife pours tea and chats amusingly to his admiring friends – is a wonderfully romantic one. Perhaps he had spent years, ever since he was a boy, picturing himself married to a beautiful, kind, gentle lady, maybe from a neighbouring village; and yet, unfortunately, the right woman (or in fact any woman at all) never came along, and so he finally gave in and advertised, and then – well, finish the story yourself. This is the joy of Lonely Hearts ads: they allow one to project upon a few short sentences a whole world of broken dreams and romance, intrigue and possibility. The image of the married couple who spend their evenings sitting blissfully together by the fireside was a potent and popular one, no doubt partly inspired by the contemporary rumour that Queen Charlotte fried sprats for her husband George III while he made toast on the fire.

Domestic virtues were increasingly revered. Many advertisers expressed a yearning to 'live in a retired domestic manner', as one put it. As the celebrated hostess and writer Mrs Elizabeth Montagu commented, 'I often think that those people are happiest who know nothing at all of the world & sitting in the little empire of the fireside, where there is no contention or cabal, think we are in a golden age of existence.' Others, however, were not quite so tactful about their need for someone to cook and clean, like the gentleman who in 1770 decided to look for a wife because he 'finds it inconvenient to leave his house to servants'.

Easily the top priority among almost all the men who advertised was that the successful candidate be aged between twenty and thirty. Being 'respectable' and 'agreeable' were also qualities that recurred frequently. Studies of human courtship have found that social skills (being 'agreeable') have always been of paramount importance in mate choice, perhaps because they suggest the ability to sustain a relationship even in the face of significant challenges. Some men were impressively modern in their demands: 'It is requested none will answer this, but who can think and act for herself' (1782). Others rated being 'accomplished' a top priority, such as the gentleman in 1776 who 'has been through France, and some part of Italy. If Fortune is so kind to join him to one that speaks another Language besides her own, it will be more agreeable; but it will be no Objection

if she does not; I will improve her.' Some, though, seemed to view
being 'accomplished' as a threat to their manhood, demanding 'that
the Lady be respectable rather than young and handsome, agreeable
in Person than in form perfect, of good Sense than distinguished
Wit, a great Mind rather than a high Spirit, and of a good Heart
than accomplished' (1791). Goodness, what a dullard! It is worth
bearing in mind, however, that none of these men were entirely
typical of their sex, otherwise they would not be approaching the
courtship process in this way in the first place.

What was new was the number of men who prized 'delicacy' or,
as one gentleman put it in an ad in the *Norwich Mercury* in 1769, 'the
more susceptible to the soft passions, the better; but this seems to
be the characteristic of the ladies here, as he was happily eye-witness
of at the theatre on a late occasion; where he observed one in particular whose very soul seemed wholly melted into tenderness, and
with whom he most feelingly sympathised'. 'Delicacy' denoted a
range of qualities, including being immensely sensitive and being
led by the heart rather than the head ('a feeling heart' was how it
was often referred to in ads), and also referred to a particular and
new form of politeness that frowned upon burping, sweating, eating
in public, even making sudden movements or mentioning bodily
functions. It was sometimes a euphemism for virginity too.

In many ways, laying claims to 'delicacy' did women no favours, as
Alexander Jardine admitted in 1788: 'Many of those female weaknesses
which we term delicacy etc., and pretend to admire, we secretly laugh
at; – or when our taste is so far vitiated as to really like them, it is
chiefly for their being symptoms of inferiority and subordination,
that soothes and feeds our pride and domineering spirit.' Certainly
many female commentators, among them Mary Wollstonecraft as
articulated in her *Vindication of the Rights of Women* (1792), suspected that
the championing of delicacy in fact intended to infantilise and under-
mine women. Yet in ads it was not only women who were ascribed
this quality, but men too: one advertiser in 1782 boasted that 'he has

a heart to offer full of affection, sensibility, and delicacy'. Indeed, according to the *Gentleman's Magazine* in 1791, 'We are every day growing more delicate, and, without doubt, at the same time more virtuous; and shall, I am confident, become the most refined and polite people in the world.' It was an aspiration, whether based in truth or not, that was repeatedly reflected in the Lonely Hearts ads of the age.

By the last quarter of the century many had tired of what they saw as the debauched nature of Georgian society and wanted to escape 'the extream of dissipation into which the age seems plunged' (1772), 'the delusive and expensive amusements of England' (1778). On a practical level, this discontent with the state of the nation was reflected in the number of men who specified that they wanted to marry someone who was 'neat, and not fantastical in her Dress' (1777). The 1770s were notorious for the outlandish fashions favoured by the aristocracy, as exemplified by Georgiana, Duchess of Devonshire, who made it fashionable to wear a drooping ostrich feather attached to the front of her enormously high wig. It was admired by some and ridiculed by many.

As the consumer revolution gained pace, the problem intensified, spreading ever further down the social scale. 'An immoderate fondness of dress' Wollstonecroft called it. Men sought a return to innocence, and therefore a wife who was 'a stranger to the hackneyed tricks of the town' (1793). It was a sentiment reflected in the literature of the age: Belinda in Maria Edgeworth's 1801 novel of the same name is commended for the way she dresses herself with 'the most perfect simplicity', in contrast to Lady Newland, who routinely appears 'Overdressed like a true city dame!'

With regards to looks, some men were very specific, such as the one who demanded a woman of 'sound Wind and Limb, Five Feet Four Inches without her Shoes; not fat, nor yet too lean; a clear Skin; sweet Breath, with good set of Teeth' (*Daily Advertiser*, 1777) – which, in evolutionary terms, are all qualities that would indicate the woman in question is likely to be fertile. However, for most men physical appearance seems not to have been a top priority, at least not one that they were prepared to admit to in the pages of a newspaper. Those who do mention it tend to be vague, employing phrases like 'good physiognomy' or 'a pleasing figure', in part because this was a society in which even to mention the human body was coming to be seen as uncouth. It makes the appearance of the phrase 'Shapely ankle preferr'd' in one ad of 1770 seem all the more risqué. Another asks simply and starkly that any prospective candidate be 'of no bodily deformity' (1772), a stipulation one is unlikely to come across in today's personal columns. One gentleman even admits that ugly is basically fine: 'As to person, easy in that choice, preferring a sweetness of temper to any personal appearance, so that irregularity in person may be acceptible' (1776).

As the rise of romantic love caused men to prioritise qualities such as 'a sweetness of temper', economic considerations were now one of a number of factors, rather than the only factor, in deciding whom to marry. This new way of thinking was reflected in the literature of the period: 'In many novels, desire for wealth with marriage marks the false values of the old: the young defy their elders' prudence to marry instead for romantic reasons . . . Yet,' adds literary critic Patricia Meyer Spacks, 'almost never do two young people propose to marry *without* financial wherewithal. Such a course seems literally inconceivable.' The perfect union would proffer a combination of love *and* money. In 1775 the newly established *Matrimonial Magazine* advised that:

> The happy marriage is, where two persons meet, and voluntarily make choice of each other, without principally regarding or neglecting the circumstance of fortune and beauty . . . Personal perfections are the only solid foundation for conjugal happiness: the gifts of fortune are adventitious, and may be acquired; but intrinsic worth is permanent and incommunicable.

The title page of the *Matrimonial Magazine* (1775): 'Cupid and Psyche in a Car drawn by a Group of Little Lovers, conducted by a youthful Hymen to the Temple of Marriage'.

Thus the writer would have approved of the gentleman in 1771 who explained that he was seeking not only a wife who possessed 'a moderate fortune', but also that 'it is a companion and a friend for life he wants, and regards not so much the outward ornaments of beauty and elegance, as the purity of the mind.'

And so romantic considerations collided with the highly commercialised world of George III's London, a world that allowed Lonely Hearts ads to thrive as never before. Money-minded, fast-paced, a rapidly increasing population: this was a city that was all about the hard sell. Everyone was on the lookout for new ways to make a quick guinea and, at the same time, the emerging middle-class was on the lookout for new ways to spend it. Just as Josiah Wedgwood advertised his teapots, so people advertised themselves. It did not matter whether goods were displayed in a shop window or on the front page of a newspaper, the effect was the same: the commercialisation of every element of the human experience, even love and marriage.

Let us be under no illusion. For many, marriage remained first and foremost a business transaction. '[A]s the advertiser is not now in business, [he] would have no objection to a widow in business in the millinery and haberdashery, mantua-making, or a genteel public house, no objection to any young person that would be agreeable to go into either of the above branches,' declared an 'agreeable, good-natured, young man, of good parents, his person and character undeniable' on the front page of the *Daily Advertiser* in 1769. Romantic love was all very well, but what use was it, if you had nowhere to live and nothing to eat? '[P]ossessed of a fortune not less than 7000l.', demands one optimistic advertiser in 1772; 'an agreeable Gentlewoman, possest [*sic*] of about fifteen hundred pounds, or a yearly income of seventy pounds,' insists another. The standard stipulation was something along the lines of 'must have a moderate and independent Fortune'.

Some revealed the reason the money is required: there is a

mortgage to be paid off or a business that needs an injection of cash. Others admitted that they were flat broke: '[The advertiser's] fortune (reduced a little by the calamities of the times) is rather small at present; but he must indisputably succeed to the posses- sion of a considerable estate immediately on the demise of a person very old and infirm . . .' read an ad in 1780, a disastrous year for many who had invested in the American colonies, which were in the midst of a full-scale revolt. Without financial means, most men found their marital options severely limited. As one bachelor asked despairingly in 1777, 'Is there a girl of moderate fortune who hath the good sense and generosity to prefer a *good* husband to a *rich* one [?]' Some ads even made the issue of the woman's dowry the opening salvo. This was a society that was blatant and robust about the economic basis of marriage, a stance reflected in many contemporary plays, novels and conduct books, where the desperate daughter forced to marry the rich husband was a common trope.

The men who did have money to offer, however, trumpeted the fact loud and clear. Many were themselves a cog in the wheel of the commercialised world of which they sought to take advantage. The 'Young man about twenty-six years, in a genteel profitable busi- ness' who advertised for a wife in the *Ledger* in the summer of 1769 was typical. Generally they were among the more successful in their field, typically specifying that the business is 'lucrative' or 'extensive' and thereby pandering to women's age-old attraction to men of means. There was also the occasional military man, and even a few MPs – exactly the sort of people who most commonly frequented coffee-houses, in fact. Some saw fit to specify their exact income, while others were a little more vague. '[O]f genteel Address, and easy circumstances' (1776) or 'blessed with an easy independence, adequate to every real comfort in life' (1793): these are just a couple of the many creative ways that people found to imply they were rich without being so vulgar as to state the fact outright. Georgian society was not ashamed to talk about money, and people sold them-selves in nakedly market terms.

Second to money, 'gentility' was the quality that men boasted of most. 'Person and character undeniable', 'of reputable connections', 'of good parents': however it was expressed, the implication was the same. Increased social mobility under George III had made it more crucial than ever to display one's genteel credentials. 'It is almost as necessary to learn a genteel behaviour and polite manners as it is to learn to speak or read or write,' the on-the-make hosier Jedediah Strutt instructed his son. With this in mind, Samuel Johnson joked about a friend of his who planned to:

> open an office in the Fleet for matrimonial panegyricks, and [who] will accommodate all with praise who think their own powers of expression inadequate to their merit. He will sell any man or woman the virtue or qualification which is most fashionable or most desired; but desires his customers to remember, that he sets beauty at the highest price, and riches at the net, and, if he be well paid, throws in virtue for nothing.

Types of men and women could now be in or out of fashion in just the same way as, say, hats. The trouble was that, to many, the very act of advertising for love contradicted all claims to gentility from the outset.

As for the other personal qualities that the men who advertised lay claim to, certain adjectives appear again and again, in partic-ular 'agreeable', 'affectionate' and 'respectable'. A 'liberal education' is a frequent boast, as is 'a good constitution'. Others tried to drum up interest by painting a picture of the kind of life that awaited the successful candidate: 'The advertiser is pleasantly situated about ten miles from town, keeps a boy and two maid servants, and raises the chief part of his provisions, and lives well in a family way'

(1782). Physical descriptions are rare, and those that do feature are vague, for instance: '[the advertiser] is not unhandsome, nor inelegant in his figure, of rather more than ordinary Stature . . .' (1791). (The qualities that men believe appeal to women have unquestionably changed considerably over the years: 'a clear head' (1777) or 'of plain person and manners' (1782) is not on many women's 'must-have' list today.)

In the last quarter of the eighteenth century, as thousands migrated to urban areas in search of work, community networks began to fragment. Many people were separated from their families and suddenly found themselves essentially rootless. Chronic loneliness was an increasingly common complaint. '[T]ired of domestic solitude,' admitted one advertiser. '[D]isgusted with the lawless unsettled state of celibacy,' lamented another. Despite what the media would have us believe, it is simply not true that everyone is out carousing and laughing and fornicating, and never has been. The vast majority of us are sitting at home in our garrets, alone and crying. As one particularly verbose advertiser put it in 1791:

> . . . when the confines of a private Life are a Barrier to our Views, and exclude the Object of our Search, while we know on the ample Plains of the Publick it is to be found, to look above the narrow Prejudices of Custom, and the more ordinary Mode of attaining our Aim, having other means in our Power, is certainly not less honourable, though more uncommon.

It is indeed difficult to meet new people in a big city. Sociologist David Riesman, in his 1950s study *The Lonely Crowd*, identified urban loneliness as a phenomenon specific to the past 300 years. There are people everywhere, and yet nowhere, creating a profound sense of isolation. Even next-door neighbours often remain strangers. The problem was most acute in London, but other cities also harboured many who, for example, had 'but a slight Acquaintance among the Female Sex', as one 'Gentleman of Property and respectable Character, who has been well brought up, under 30, healthy, and well situated in Business' explained to readers of *Aris's Gazette*, Birmingham's foremost newspaper, in 1797.

In general, men turned to Lonely Hearts ads as a last resort after having no luck elsewhere: 'It may occasion surprize, that a Gentleman of good fortune and connections should have recourse to advertizement, for obtaining what might be imagined he could have procured without it; but not having yet found an object entirely to his liking, he was determined to try this mode, however singular and disadvantageous' (1790). In an era when divorce was almost impossible, it was essential to choose one's partner wisely: 'Matrimony, my dear, is like a mouse trap, it is easy to get into, but hard to get out of.' For some, 'a most excessive timidity' was the problem; others had recently returned from abroad. Many simply worked too hard. In the summer of 1794, a Lonely Hearts ad was placed in the *Morning Chronicle* from 'A reputable tradesman in the neighbourhood of Bond-street, about thirty-five years of age, in a genteel and profitable business which clears at present about 200l per annum . . .' He was typical of the sort who advertised, not a loser with no friends, but someone who was just too busy to have a social life: 'The advertiser, from his uniform application to business, has not had an opportunity of being much in the company of the fair sex, which induces him to take this method of addressing his sentiments.' This was an enormously common complaint, shared in particular by men in the armed forces: 'A Gentleman of a good Family, Rank, and liberal Education, who is at present in the military line, which he would be happy to quit, as it deprives him of the felicity of making agreeable acquaintances amongst Ladies of good families and fortune . . .' (1782).

Lonely Hearts ads were also popular among those in a hurry. In 1798, a Hungerford yeoman named Timothy Surrell announced to readers of the *Reading Mercury* not only that he wished to marry ('she must be genteel made, rather tall; black, brown, flaxen, or auburn hair; age from twenty-five to thirty-five'), but also that 'To avoid extra expenses, Mr Surrell would wish to keep his wedding and harvest-home the same evening, which will be within fourteen days from the present date, as he particularly wishes the lady to preside at table this evening.' Not the most romantic of offers.

A standard Lonely Hearts lexicon gradually evolved. Ads were invariably written in the third person, which allowed the author to detach himself from the text and present it as if it were news: 'Stop press! Man wants wife!', as it were. Certain phrases appear again and again – 'Discretion assured', 'letters post paid' – but the language tends to be relatively straightforward, and no abbreviations of the 'G.S.O.H.' sort are employed; in the same way, there is little creativity or jokiness in the composition. 1772 saw one of the first witty headlines of the kind that are so common today: 'A Bold Stroke for a good Wife', it read, a reference to the Susanna Centlivre play of 1717, *A Bold Stroke for a Wife*. Thus it grabbed the reader's attention, emulating the type of tricks that advertisers had been using elsewhere for some time, and enabling the language of consumption to creep into the private sphere.

In 1785, London's nine daily newspapers were joined by yet another, the *Universal Daily Register*, later known as *The Times*. From the outset, its founder, John Walter, sought to encourage all kinds of ads, from:

> masters who wants servants, or servants masters; traders, who wish to buy or sell goods; the fair, whether maids or widows, who sigh for husbands and help-mates; in a word, all sorts and sizes, denominations and descriptions of men, have nothing to do but advertise in the *Universal Register* – and they will immediately hear something to their advantage.

Within a couple of years, *The Times* had made its first foray into the
world of Lonely Hearts ads – albeit in jest.

On 17 October 1786, an ad appeared supposedly from a woman
on the hunt for a husband. Her sight, she claimed, was not very
good due to an accident she had suffered some years back, which
had left her face badly burnt – the implication being that she was
very ugly. There is no reason to doubt that the replies to 'the Burnt
Lady' that the newspaper received, and later printed, were genuine,
and so they provide a rare body of evidence about the sort of letters
that an ad like this elicited.

The answer is: all sorts. A few demanded to know whether the
advertiser was genuine before they deigned to offer up any details
about themselves. One letter arrived from a twenty-four-year-old
with an income of £80 a year, who implausibly claimed that 'it has
always been my determination never to marry what is called a handsome woman, for the most part of them are so exceedingly vain,
that all their time is taken up in adorning their persons, leaving the
mind, which is the essential part, totally barren and unadorned'.
Another was written in the form of twenty rhyming couplets and
posted in Hoxton, hence one suspects it originated from the boys'
boarding school there. The most serious candidate for matrimony
was a twenty-six-year-old lawyer, 'sober, yet cheerful and active . . .
religious and sincere . . . a good figure and a proportionable man'.
The Burnt Lady was said to be keen on him, but 'she will dispense
with any further address, as, in taking a turn upon Hampstead
Heath the other morning, the spiteful East wind has opened a small
watery tumour in her face, which will oblige her, for some time, to
wear a mask'.

A couple of months later, the top of the second column of page
one of the newspaper (which by this time was where all the personal
ads were printed) featured a gem of an ad from 'A Gentleman of
very considerable fortune, about the age of forty' who, '[t]hough he
possesses an excellent and unimpaired constitution, is afflicted with

MONDAY, DECEMBER 11, 1786.

PANTHEON,
DECEMBER 9th, 1786.

THE Nobility and Gentry are respectfully acquainted that there will be a CONCERT at this Place, TO-MORROW, the 11th Inst. and be continued on every succeeding Tuesday during the season.

The Vocal Parts by Messrs. Arrowsmith, Sale, Billington, Chapman, Salmon, Sirton, and Mrs. Barthelemon.

The Orchestra under the Direction of Mr. Barthelemon.

The BAND is improved and a great variety of new Music, as Songs, Glees, Overtures, Concertos, &c. &c. will be performed during the Season.

Admittance Three Shillings and Sixpence each Person or Tickets may be had at the Office.

Refreshments as usual.

The Doors will be opened at Eight o'Clock, and the Concert begin at Nine.

MATRIMONY.

A Gentleman of very considerable fortune, about the age of forty, offers himself as an Husband to any well-educated, amiable and agreeable Lady, of good character and not more than thirty years of age, and as much younger as may be, who will undertake to exercise those attentions which his particular situation requires. Though he possesses an excellent and unimpaired constitution, he is afflicted with an incurable weakness in his knees, occasioned by the kick of an Ostrich, in the East Indies, which disables him from walking, rising from his chair, or getting from his bed, without assistance. That assistance he wishes to receive from the tender care of an affectionate young Lady. Fortune is not an object of his consideration.

Letters addressed to M. P. at Mr. Wallis's, Printseller, Ludgate-street; will receive every proper attention. No other enquiry need be made, as no information can be given.

FELL from DYDE's, Pall-Mall,
AND,
WILLIAM's from HARTSHORN's, Wig-more-street.

RESPECTFULLY acquaint the Nobility, Gentry, and Public in general, that they have opened a Warehouse, at No. 15, Mount-street, Grosvenor-square, in the Millinery, Haberdashery, Fur and Glove Trades; which will be sold on the very lowest terms, for ready money, and they hope by a constant assiduity and attention, which shall ever be paid to their kind encouragers, to give every satisfaction, which nothing in their power shall be wanting to procure.

A Variety of fashionable spotted, Fox, Lynx, Bear, Racoon, &c. Muffs, Black, Leather, and white monk Ermine, at 3s. each. Ladies long and habit gloves 11d. per pair, stamp included; crape gauzes, from 10d. per yard, upwards; real yard wide crape, 3s. 6d. per yard; ell-wide

---

Without Deception or Equivocation.

TWO PRIZES to a BLANK,
And TWO to ONE that the Adventurer cannot Lose.

MR. SHERGOLD, No. 50, Lombard-Street, and No. 117, Fleet-Street, having no concern with any other Office in London, respectfully thanking his numerous subscribers in the IRISH LOTTERY, for their encomiums upon the plan in the execution of which he was intrusted, requests their attention to Two Systems which will equally meet their approbation, as they will bear the investigation of the discerning, and coincide with his maxim, never to attempt a delusion, by describing, under any masque or reservations, advantages which do not in reality exist.

The FIRST SUBSCRIPTION
Is in Two Divisions, at ONE GUINEA and HALF-a-GUINEA, and literally contains TWO PRIZES to One BLANK; for if it is drawn on or before the Twenty-second Day of Drawing, being about Two Thirds of the whole Drawing, the Subscriber of ONE GUINEA will receive

£.	if	£.	if	£.
1250		20,000	40		2,000
600	—	10,000	20	—	500
300	—	5,000	4	—	100
100	—	2,000	2	—	50

ONE GUINEA, the whole Subscription, if a Prize of £20.

ONE GUINEA, the whole Subscription, if a BLANK.

Every Adventurer must see that he has the Benefits upon the capital Prizes of a Sixteenth Share, which costs ONE GUINEA, with this MATERIAL DISTINCTION, that in the Share he has TWO BLANKS to a Prize, and in SHERGOLD's Subscription TWO PRIZES to a Blank. It is beyond all cavil or argument, that the Adventurer cannot lose but by the Ticket remaining undrawn after the Twenty-second Day, against which the Chances are TWO to One. This computation is founded upon a review of all Lotteries of 50,000 Tickets, which, when no accident has intervened, have been commonly concluded in periods from Twenty-nine to Thirty-four Days.

For HALF-a-GUINEA

The Subscriber will receive exactly Half the Benefit of those at ONE GUINEA, with TWO to One also in his Favour, that he does not lose even HALF-a-GUINEA, after having a Chance for all the CAPITAL PRIZES.

SECOND SUBSCRIPTION

Attended with a clear and evident Saving of Fifty per Cent. being a SIXTEENTH Share for FOURTEEN SHILLINGS instead of ONE GUINEA, is in TWO DIVISIONS at FOURTEEN SHILLINGS and SEVEN SHILLINGS for the WHOLE TIME of DRAWING, and including every Prize whatever.

The Subscriber of FOURTEEN SHILLINGS will receive

£.	if	£.	if	£.
1250	—	20,000	62 10		1,000

The Times, 11 December 1786

an incurable weakness in his knees, occasioned by the kick of an
Ostrich, in the East Indies, which disables him from walking, rising
from his chair, or getting from his bed, without assistance. That
assistance he wishes to receive from the tender care of an affectionate young Lady.' The ad adheres to the standard lexicon of the
genre, even including a mention of John Wallis, who was a well-
known London bookseller. At first glance it is in every way
convincing, indeed compelling, with the vivid reference to 'the kick
of an Ostrich, in the East Indies'. The only problem is that there
were no ostriches in the East Indies during this period. Thus the
suspicion is that it was written by Walter himself to fill space, enter-
tain readers and perhaps even drum up genuine ads of a similar
kind. Like John Houghton before him, he had spotted the commercial possibilities inherent in the marriage market and sought to
exploit them.

   But genuine Lonely Hearts ads did appear in *The Times*, albeit
only occasionally, as did 'Once Seen' ads. They were invariably jostled
on the page by other ads for all types of other commodities. The
one that appeared in *The Times* on 2 October 1795, from 'A Young
Gentleman of Fortune, who is well-established in a reputable
Mercantile Business, of a pleasing figure and address, and good
disposition' in search of 'an accomplished LADY of a congenial
mind, from 17 to 22 years of age, of lively and engaging manners,
of a reputable family, and with an adequate fortune, independent
of brothers and sisters', was surrounded by a typically disparate
group of ads for everything from a gentleman looking for lodgings
(preferably 'an airy situation, small Family and clean neat House')
to the sale of some 'clean, healthy, trained peach and nectarine trees'
and a cure for venereal disease. It is the story of a metropolis printed
in smudged black ink. The newspaper had replaced the marketplace
as the principal public forum where people shared information,
made connections and formed alliances.

TWO HUNDRED to TWO HUNDRED and FIFTY GUINEAS will be given to any Lady or Gentleman having interest to procure a permanent. PLACE for the Advertiser, aged 25, from 60l. to 100l. per annum. Salary not so much the object, if for life. Secrecy may be relied on.
Address for Mr. N. at Mr. Starby's; No. 52, Castle-street, Southwark, or at No. 24, Duke-street, St. James's.

CO-PARTNERSHIP.

WANTED, in an established, ready money, and respectable Manufactory, about 25 miles West of London, a PARTNER who can command 3000l. He may either act or not, in the management of the business, as may be most agreeable to himself. The profits on the capital are at least 20 per Cent.
Particulars may be known by applying to Mr. Kibblewhite, Gray's-Inn Place.

WANTED, for a single Gentleman, LODGINGS neatly furnished, near the Exchange, not further Westward than Cheapside; to consist of two good Sitting-rooms and a Bed-chamber, or Dressing-room on the first floor, and two good Bed-chambers above, if the Dressing-room is on the first floor, or one good Bed-chamber on the first floor, and another above, if the Dressing-room be there. Preference will be given to an airy situation, small Family, and clean neat House.
Letters directed to X. Y. No. 41, Cornhill, mentioning size and apartments, rent, number in family, and such other particulars as may serve to convey a distinct idea of the accommodations (in order to save trouble to both parties), will be answered, if the apartments are likely to suit.

WANTED, for a Term of about 99 Years, from 40 to 100 Acres of Arable and Pasture LAND (on some part of which it is intended to build a Villa and Offices), near the Banks of the Thames, distant from London 15 to about 40 miles, in some agreeable and picturesque situation, commanding a variegated and pleasant landscape; and if there is an old Mansion on the Premises it will be the more agreeable, in the neighbourhood of Henley, Wallingford, Long Ditton, Taplow Hill, Maidenhead Hill, Egham, Chertsey, or any part of Windsor Forest.
Any person having such Land to Let, are desired to send terms and particulars to Mr. Thomas, Architect, No. 29, Alsop's Buildings, New Road.

WANTED immediately, in a healthy, airy, public, and lively situation, within the town, or a mile from it, furnished or unfurnished, for two or three years or upwards, a new and nearly built HOUSE, of two stories high besides the ground floor, with two rooms on each, kitchen under ground, with every convenience, a pond, or running water in plenty; and a large walled garden, well planted and stocked. A fair rent, according to circumstances, will be allowed. The Advertiser has no children nor family, and the house to be kept in good condition
Address to Mr. D. R. No. 196, Houndsditch. A line, with description of the house, will be duly attended to.

TO be LET, in a pleasant airy situation at Islington, for a single Lady or Gentleman, a FIRST FLOOR, genteely furnished; and a Lady or Gentleman wanted to Board in a family way.
Enquire at No. 30, Cofswell-street.

ST. JAMES's.

TO be LET, a genteel HOUSE, situate at the entrance of St. James's Place, the first door on the right hand from St. James's-street.
Enquire on the Premises; or at No. 44, Howland-street, Fitzroy-square.

TO be LET, Furnished, a HOUSE in the vicinity of Portman-square, fit for the immediate reception of a genteel family.
To be viewed with tickets only, which may be had by applying to Mr. Rawlings, Upholder, No. 27, Red Lion-square.

TO be LET, a HOUSE in Sloane-street, Knightsbridge, very well furnished, till Christmas or longer. Terms no object, provided the parties be approved, and the Furniture taken care of. Two or three Ladies might find it very pleasant, as the family to whom it belongs might be occasionally in the house, and happy in their domesticating together.
Address or enquire for M. M. at M. and H. Smith's Circulating Library, No 5, Sloane-street. None but those of respectability need apply.

TO be SOLD, a number of clean, healthy, trained PEACH and NECTARINE TREES of the best forts, four years old; also some of an older and larger growth.
Enquire at the Phoenix Inn, Isleworth, Middlesex.

MATRIMONY.

A YOUNG GENTLEMAN of Fortune, who is well-established in a reputable Mercantile Business, of a pleasing figure and address, and good disposition, is solicitous for an introduction to an accomplished LADY of a congenial mind, from 17 to 22 years of age, of lively and engaging manners, of a reputable family, and with an adequate fortune, independent of brothers and sisters.
A line addressed to C. B. City Coffee-house, Cheapside, will meet with the most respectful attention, and inviolable secrecy.

This day is published, price 2s.

A PRACTICAL TREATISE on the Good and Bad Effects of SEA BATHING. By JOHN ANDERSON, M.D. F.A.S. C.M.S. &c. Physician to and a Director of the General Sea Bathing Infirmary at Margate.
Printed for C. Dilly, and Murray, London; and S. Silver, Margate. Where may be had, by the same Author, a Preliminary Introduction to the Act of Sea Bathing, 1s.

SALES BY AUCTION.

LINEN-DRAPERY and FURNITURE, Newgate-street.
By Mr. WINSTANLEY,
THIS DAY, on the Premises, No. 61, Newgate-street, at 11 o'Clock,

THE Remaining STOCK in TRADE, HOUSEHOLD FURNITURE, Plate, Linen, China, Books, Paintings, and Prints, amongst which is a capital Subscription Impression of the Death of General Wolfe, and other Effects, of Mr. GILBERT BURN, Linen-draper, retiring from Business. The Stock consists of Muslins, Dimities, Irish Linens and Sheetings, printed and plain Callicoes, Shawls, Handkerchiefs, and other Goods, which will be lotted suitable for private Families, as well as the Trade.
To be viewed on Wednesday, when Catalogues may be had on the Premises; and of Mr. Winstanley, Paternoster Row.

LEASEHOLDS, Hoxton, & FREEHOLDS, Spitalfields.
By Mr. SMITH,
At Mr. Warbrack's, the Hare, Hoxton, THIS DAY, at 12 o'clock,

THREE compact FREEHOLD DWELLING HOUSES, forming the whole of New-court, Dorset-street, Spitalfields, in the occupation of Mrs. Hendry, Mr. Styles, &c. at rents amounting to 22l. per annum. Two Leasehold Dwelling-houses and Gardens, pleasantly situate in Turner's-square, Hoxton, let to Messrs. Sharratt and Simpson, at rents amounting to 18l. 8s. per annum; and three Leasehold Dwelling-houses, with Gardens to each, eligibly situate, Nos. 2, 3, and 4, in Monk's-buildings, Coffee-house-walk, Hoxton, let to Messrs. Humblebee, Wicks, and Homewood, at rents amounting to 29l.9s. per annum.
May be viewed by leave of the tenants, and particulars had 6 days preceding the Sale, at the Hare, Hoxton; and of Mr. Smith, No. 62, Broad-street.

FREEHOLD ESTATE, within two Miles of Tunbridge-Wells.—By Mr. CHEESEMAN,
At the Sussex Tavern, Tunbridge-Wells, on Wednesday, Oct. 7, at 12 o'Clock,

A FREEHOLD ESTATE called ELYES, consisting of a HOUSE in the most perfect repair, fit for the accommodation of a moderate Family, with convenient Offices, together with 60 Acres of Land contiguous, all in grass, and divided into several inclosures. It is a healthy spot, and the pleasantness of the situation cannot be exceeded
Enquire of Mr. Cheeseman; or Mr. Jones, Attorney at Law, Tunbridge-Wells; or of Mr. Phillips, Carpenter, in Mount-street.

NEWBOTTLE, NORTHAMPTONSHIRE.
By Mr. YOUNG,
In several Lots, at the Red Lion, in Banbury, in November next, unless disposed of by Private Contract before the 15th of October, 1795, in one Lot,

A Valuable and very desirable FREEHOLD ESTATE, consisting of the MANORS of NEWBOTTLE and CHARLTON, with the ancient Mansion, and sundry capital Farms and Woodlands in hand, containing 820 Acres of rich enclosed Land, lying perfectly compact in a ring fence, and let tythe-free to respectable tenants at will. Also, the Great Tythes of the Parish of Newbottle, and the Advowson of the Vicarage; the present Rental upwards of 800l. The situation of the whole Estate is only about 6 miles from Banbury, and is peculiarly adapted for a Sportsman, the Manors being very extensive, and well stocked with game, and also well wooded and watered.
Printed Particulars may be had of Messrs. Bignell and

A Lonely Hearts ad in *The Times*, 2 October 1795

THURSDAY, DECEMBER 18, 1800.

A CARD.—If the Lady who a Gentleman handed into her carriage from Covent Garden Theatre, on Wednesday the third of this month, will oblige the Advertiser with a line to Z.Z. Spring Garden Coffee House, saying if married or single, she will quiet the mind of a young Nobleman, who has tried, but in vain, to find the Lady. The carriage was ordered to Bond-street. The Lady may depend on honour and secrecy.—Nothing but the most honourable interview is intended. The Lady was in mourning, and sufficiently clouthed to distinguish her for possessing every virtue and charm that man could desire in a female that he would make choice of for a Wife. Deception will be detected, as the Lady's person can never be forgot.

ONE HUNDRED POUNDS will be given to any Lady or Gentleman who can procure for a young Man of respectability a SITUATION in any of the Public Offices. Secrecy will be observed. Address to A.L. Antigallican Coffeehouse, Threadneedle-street.

TRAVELLER.—A Person of Address, who has travelled many years for Houses of the first respectability, and whose character will stand the strictest scrutiny, wishes to form a connection above a respectable House who may wish to push a Country Trade in any of the following lines of business :—Wines and Spirits, Teas and Sugar, Vinegar, Soap, Blue, and Starch, Oils, Hops, British Wines, Tobacco and Snuff, &c. &c.—Address Letters for B. E. London Coffee-house.—N. B. The Advertiser, amongst other things, is a judge of Wines and Spirits, and in that line of business knows every transaction at the Custom-house, Excise, and on the Keys.

CLERKSHIP.—A young Man of respectability, who has a superficial knowledge of Trade in general, and thoroughly acquainted with the Continental Languages, wishes to engage himself as CLERK in a Mercantile House at Home, or as Rider or Traveller, either on the Continent or at Home. Having been most accustomed to the Wine Trade, would prefer it. Address to E.E.K. No. 51, Burr-street.—Ireland would be preferred, and the West Indies not objected to.

WANTED, an APPRENTICE in the Grocery Line, in one of the first Shops of respectability and business, in the West End of the Town ; a Youth of genteel connections ; he will be respected as one of the family, as are the present young men. A handsome Premium will be expected. Apply at No. 36, Holborn.

WANTED to PURCHASE, the immediate PRESENTATION to a LIVING in Hants, Berks, or Surry, from 300l. to 500l. per Annum. The neighbourhood of Reading would be preferred. Address (post paid) to A.B.C. Post Office, Hartford-Bridge, Hants ; or Printing-office, High-street, Oxford.

TO any LADY going to BENGAL.—A BLACK WOMAN, of good character, returning to India, would be glad to attend on a Lady, and to have the care of Children, having been accustomed to the above situations. Apply to No. 31, Finsbury-square.

TO Wholesale LINEN-DRAPERS, HABERDASHERS, HOSIERS, &c.—WANTS a SITUATION as TRAVELLER, a middle-aged Person, that has been constantly engaged therein for 20 years past, and possesses an extensive Country connection, with a thorough knowledge of the business. Address to R.O. City Coffee-house, Cheapside.

TO WHOLESALE or RETAIL TRADERS and MANUFACTURERS, in Town or Country—WANTS a SITUATION, an experienced CASH and BOOK-KEEPER, a married person, nearly 30 years of age, who is acquainted with double entry, and competent to plan, or follow such methods as are suitable to particular branches of business. He has lived with persons of respectability, who can give the most satisfactory account of his conduct, dispatch, and accuracy, and has been in the practice of annually balancing a partnership concern of some magnitude. He can give requisite security, and is willing to make the

THE CORPORATION of the TOWN of SHREWSBURY being desirous of enlarging the SUPPLY of WATER for the Use of the Inhabitants, from Brockwell Springs, situated about one mile and a half South West of the Town, will give a Premium of THIRTY POUNDS to the Person who shall, in the judgment of the Corporation, point out the most eligible method, together with an Estimate of the Expence, of conveying 1900 gallons per hour, and of distributing the same, in the most convenient, compleat, and economical manner, to various parts of the Town. A Plan and Section of the Direction of the present Pipe may be seen at the Town Clerk's Office, where all Proposals must be sent, sealed up, on or before the 5th day of January 1800. LOXDALE, Town Clerk.

GRAND JUNCTION CANAL WHARF, WHITEFRIARS.—CARRIAGE by LAND and WATER.—The WARWICK BOAT COMPANY beg leave to inform the Public, that they regularly once a Week, or oftener, load a STAGE BOAT at the above Wharf, for the under-mentioned Places ; and that all Goods committed to their care will meet with every possible dispatch, by their Agent, Mr. E. Bottomley, of whom, on application as above, further particulars may be had : Daventry, Southam, Kenilworth, Shipston, Stratford on Avon, Wallboum, Warwick, Birmingham, Wolverhampton, Walsall, Wednesbury, Bilston, Dudley, Tepston, Stourbridge, Burton on Trent, Fazeley, Tamworth, and all intermediate Places.—They also take Goods in, three Days a Week, at the above Places, for London, particulars of which may be had, by applying to either Mr. Weston, Stourbridge ; Mr. Bett, Birmingham ; or Mr. suffolk, at the Company's Office, Warwick.

NOTICE to CREDITORS.—The Creditors (if any) upon the ESTATE of JOHN WATTS, late of Honiton, in the County of Devon, Esq. deceased, but formerly of Buckleysbury, in the City of London, Merchant, are desired to send their Claims, on or before the 20th day of January next, to Mr. Reader Wilkinson, of the Minories, Druggist ; or Mr. Emanuel Muller, of Lawrence Pountney-lane, Merchant, two of the Executors of the deceased ; or to Mr. C. Flood, Attorney at Law, of Honiton aforesaid, otherwise they will be precluded from all Benefit of the said Estate. And all persons who may be indebted to the said Estate are desired forthwith to pay such Debts to the said Executors, or to Mr. Flood.

TO be RE-SOLD, pursuant to an Order of the High Court of Chancery, bearing date the 19th day of November, 1800, and made in a Cause entitled Williams and others against Bird and others, on the 15th day of Jan. 1801, between the hours of 1 and 2 o'clock in the afternoon, at the Public Sale Room of the said Court, in Southampton-buildings Chancery-lane, London, before Peter Holford, Esq. one of the Masters of the said Court, a ROPE WALK, situate at or near Stepney-Causeway, in the Parish of Stepney, in the County of Middlesex, with a good Dwelling-house, Garden, and Pasture Grounds, let on lease to Mr. Norrison Coverdale. Particulars whatever may be had, gratis, at the said Master's Chambers in Southampton-buildings ; of Mr. Millard, Cordwainer's-Hall ; Messrs. Williamsand Brooks, Lincoln's Inn ; Messrs. Collins and Reynolds, Spital-square ; Mr. Robins, Gray's Inn-place ; and of Mr. Parkinson, Symond's Inn.

TO be PEREMPTORILY SOLD, in two Lots, pursuant to a Decree and Order of the High Court of Chancery, made in a Cause, Saunders v. Martin, before John Simeon, Esq. one of the Masters of the said Court, at the Public Sale Room of the Court, in Southampton-Buildings, Chancery-lane, London, on the 19th day of January next, between the hours of five and six in the afternoon, PART of the ESTATE, late of WILLIAM SKYNNER, Esq. deceased, consisting of a capital Messuage or Dwelling-house, and 383 acres of Land, with the barns, stables, water, corn, grist mill, and other buildings thereunto belonging, called Vaynor and Pontshane Mill, in the Parish of Llawhaden, in the County of Pembroke. Also a Rent Charge of 200l. per annum, payable for ever, out of a Freehold Estate called Weston, in the said County, worth 150l. per annum.—Particulars may be had (gratis) at the said Master's Chambers, in

A 'Once Seen' ad in *The Times*, 18 December 1800

The coffee-house lay at the heart of the Lonely Hearts business. Many well-known ones appear in ads, such as the Cocoa Tree (where the aforementioned M.L. asked that letters be addressed) and the Chapter (where the Brontës later stayed), but what is really striking is the sheer number of coffee-houses that are referred to, many of which have since disappeared from the record, perhaps just fly-by-night ventures. An invention of the 1650s, by the middle of the next century coffee-houses were past their heyday, no longer quite as glamorous and fashionable as they used to be, but simply an everyday element of London's landscape. Their new role included acting as a clearing house for those who dreamed of wedded bliss. Many people were introduced to ads via the newspapers they read there – proprietors encouraged custom by taking out subscriptions to a number of publications, and letting everyone read them free of charge – but it was also often the location chosen for replies to be received, and even occasionally for the first meeting. Most coffee-houses were in the City, Covent Garden, Fleet Street or the area around St James's, and they were known for their relatively diverse clientele. 'What a lesson to see a lord, or two, a baronet, a shoe-maker, a tailor, a wine-merchant and a few others of the same stamp poring over the same newspaper,' marvelled the French writer Abbé Prévost. Like most, Prévost assumed that all those who were 'poring' over the papers were in search of news of the latest victory in France or aristocratic scandal. Perhaps, however, they were hunting for a bedfellow.

It was not just coffee-houses that were implicated in the intrigue of Lonely Hearts ads. There was Mrs Slater's (a haberdasher's near Leicester Square), Mr Wheble's (a bookseller's opposite St Dunstan's on Fleet Street), Mr Pignaud's (a perfumer's on Berners Street), Mr William's (a shoemaker's on Berners Street). As one trawls through the ads, one gets a vivid sense of London as a hive of commercial activity. By the end of the century, Oxford Street alone boasted 153 shops, each one a new potential public place at which to receive letters furtively. Pubs like the Horn Tavern on Fleet Street and the Nag's Head in Walthamstow fulfilled a similar function for a rather less salubrious class of advertiser. And the offices of the newspaper itself were another popular option. Did John Walter (or either of his sons, who succeeded him as editor) learn to spot those who arrived at the newspaper's offices off Gray's Inn Road with the intention of placing a Lonely Hearts ad? A nervous smile, a palpable urge to take care of business quickly, an air of shiftiness compared to those who were there to publicise a house for sale or a cure for venereal disease might all have been a clue.

Most must fervently have hoped that Walter was not watching. The appeal of coffee-houses, pubs and newspapers offices was the anonymity they offered. Many ads now concluded with a phrase such as 'She may depend on the strictest secrecy being observed.' As a consequence, it was less likely than ever that couples who met in this way would leave a trail of evidence behind them for the twenty-first-century historian to uncover. On the rare occasion that an ad did feature the advertiser's full name, it almost always seems to have been invented. For instance, in 1776 an ad placed by one 'M. Middleton' – 'a batchelor, aged 42 … free from the use of the Indian weed, temperate in way of living, and not inclinable to a midnight conversation, though cheerfully enjoys his friends' – asked all those who considered themselves wife material to write to him care of the Belvedere, a pub in Islington. But a visit to the Public Record Office reveals, alas, no great eighteenth-century love story. There is no record of a forty-something Mr Middleton, let alone of his marital history. This does not mean he did not exist, but it does suggest that the ad was not entirely genuine (the phrase 'free from the use of the Indian weed' may also be a clue).

There is no doubt that such couples did exist, however. In 1784, a gentleman calling himself 'Asiaticus' wrote a long letter to the *Edinburgh Courant* in which he declared, 'I have often heard matrimonial ads ridiculed; but I know two of the happiest matches, perhaps, in the island, which were formed by a letter in the news-papers.' And so he decided to give it a go himself. His perfect woman would not only possess 'a well-turned and delicate mind', but would also be:

> so well informed as to make a conversible companion; but she must not have been an indiscriminate reader, especially at circu-lating libraries, as I would not have her mind either corrupted or giddy with extravagant views of life. I would have her accus-tomed to simple, chaste, and elegant manners; not possessing the half-breeding of vulgar opulence, nor used to the free manners of dissipated high life. I would rather look for her in the bosom of retirement, practising every domestic virtue and amiable accomplishment, than in the haunts of dissipation, gaiety, and folly. I would wish her to possess rather a mild and gentle temper than a quick and very lively disposition ...

'Asiaticus' concludes this depressing list of qualities with one final, inevitable demand: she should be aged between twenty and thirty.

A fortnight later 'Asiaticus' wrote to the newspaper again, this time to inform readers that his ad had had a very happy outcome: 'By your means I have been introduced to the correspondence of Laura, whose character, manners, and accomplishments, lead me to the most flattering prospects of happiness.' He explains that, in his search for a wife, he was 'led to a mode of application which would perhaps be reckoned uncommon' by dint of 'being so long a stranger to my native country'. Not surprisingly, he was now a big fan of Lonely Hearts ads: 'Were such a method more frequently practised, it might be the means of bringing many worthy characters together, whose minds are fitted for each other, but whom accident or unac-quaintance keep asunder. – I have several acquaintances, richer and more deserving than myself, but similar in other respects, whom I shall advise to follow my example.'

His touchingly sentimental bent is indicative of the rise of romantic love in the Georgian era. It is 'happiness', not money, that he dreams of. Yet to me what really stands out from his letter is the all-too-fleeting mention of Laura. Who is Laura? What are her 'character, manners, and accomplishments'? Where is her voice in all this?

Chapter Four

Sighs and Lamentations

IT WAS THE second day of a new year – 1788 – a time when even the most cheerful among us are prone to feeling a little low and in need of some friendly companionship, and as London's genteel class sat down to the breakfast table and opened up their newspapers, the front page of *The Times* confronted them with a startling plea for help:

MATRIMONY.

A Lady, about 25 years of age, who has been flattered with the idea of possessing an agreeable person, and who, without any flattery at all, is in the actual possession of an independent fortune,—solicits the attention of any young gentleman of birth, education, and personal consequence. The ill usage of her relations has obliged her to separate herself from them; and they, in revenge, not only employ their utmost malice to disturb her repose, but threaten prosecutions to deprive her of her fortune.

Any such Gentleman, therefore, who will stand forth as her protector, to save her from the tyranny of her family on the one hand, and the impositions of lawyers on the other, shall be rewarded with the object he has protected, and the fortune he has preserved.

Letters addressed for Eleonora, at Mr. Mutc.ius's, Charing-cross, will have due attention.

The Times, 2 January 1788

It reads like a predicament dreamed up by a lady novelist; and yet, assuming the ad is to be taken at face value, it is a vivid snapshot of one woman trying to stay afloat in a harsh world.

We have no way of knowing the true identity of the troubled Eleonora, but what is certain is that she was not the only member of her sex to find that Georgian Britain had dealt her a duff set of cards. The most striking element of Lonely Hearts ads placed by women in this period is the sense of desperation that emanates off the page. There is the 'young Lady, who has lost her husband, and whose family affairs oblige her to be from her friends . . .' (1777), the 'Young Lady [who] is desirous of freeing herself from the control of a cruel and capricious Guardian' (1781), the 'Woman of Character, under misfortunes' (1790), the 'young Person . . . compelled by loss of Friends and severe Misfortunes to solicit Protection' from 'the most poignant sufferings' (1802); and this is in addition to the many widows and orphans who reveal themselves to be in 'distressed circumstances'. Even bearing in mind that women's experiences were diverse and complex and that one must be wary of generalisations, the picture that emerges is sad – and, at the same time, amazingly courageous.

For most women, marriage was the be-all and end-all. The idea that they might miss out on this sacred state was viewed with dread: 'I have a Mortal Aversion to be an Old Maid, and a decaid Oak before my Window, leaveless, half rotten, and shaking its wither'd Top, puts me in Mind every morning of an Antiquated Virgin, Bald, with Rotten Teeth, and shaking of the Palate,' wrote the future Lady Mary Wortley Montagu near the beginning of the eighteenth century. As women approached adulthood, Georgian society presented them with few options, both financially and otherwise. And as the average age at which women got married fell, from just over twenty-six in 1700 to just over twenty-three in 1800, the pressure to conform intensified accordingly.

The majority of women met their future husband through friends or family. Who to marry was often the most important decision they ever made. In 1742, Kentish gentlewoman Mary Warde warned that 'No Woman of understanding can marry without infinite apprehensions, such a step inconsiderately taken discovers a Levity and Temper that is always displeasing to a looker on . . . & if the woman has the good fortune to meet with a man that uses her well it is being happy so much by chance that she does not deserve it.' It was frightening the role that 'chance' played, especially in view of what a serious step marriage was, resulting as it did in the transfer of all a woman's property to her husband, who would also have custody of any ensuing children (this remained the case right up until 1875). It was entirely legal to beat or imprison one's wife, and divorce was almost impossible: of the 325 divorces between 1670 and 1857 (every one of which required its own Act of Parliament), only four were granted to women.

Thus the search for a husband tended to dominate a young woman's waking hours. Without one, it was extremely difficult to support oneself financially. As Mrs Reeves lamented in Samuel Richardson's novel *Sir Charles Grandison* (1753–4), 'I believe many a poor girl goes up the hill with a companion she would little care for, if the state of a single woman were not here so peculiarly unprovided and helpless.' True, those towards the bottom of the social scale could usually find work as a domestic or farm servant, or could set themselves up in a trade such as wool-spinning or (increasingly from the 1770s onwards, when the introduction of the spinning jenny resulted in wool-spinning's dramatic decline) lace-making, straw-plaiting or glove-making. Some had their own business – millinery, mantua-making or running an inn, perhaps – while others were forced to turn to rather less respectable professions such as acting or prostitution. Among the genteel sort, however, the options were more limited. They could continue to live at home with their parents or siblings, in return for being at everyone's beck and call at a moment's notice. Or they could try to find a position as a governess, a lady's companion or a teacher, which were among the few jobs deemed respectable. As Mary Wollstonecraft commented in *Thoughts on the Education of Daughters* (1787), 'Few are the modes of earning a subsistence and those very humiliating.'

'Single women have a dreadful propensity for being poor – which is one very strong argument in favour of Matrimony', wrote Jane Austen to her niece. It was rare to remain single by choice, and while some women proved easy to matchmake (Georgiana Spencer was married off to the Duke of Devonshire at the age of seventeen), others found it rather more difficult to elicit a marriage proposal. And so it was that the boldest among them pursued alternative avenues in the hope of finding their Mr Right – or, more realistically, their Mr Anyone. Not all could afford it: placing an ad cost between two and three shillings, so it was an option available only to those of a middle-class station or above who had access to money of their own. Lonely Hearts ads from women are inevitably fewer than those from men, but they do exist and are a rare example of female needs and desires being committed to paper (assuming that the ads were indeed authored by the women they described; it is likely that many turned to a friend, sister or trusted maid for help in composing the all-important few sentences).

One of the earliest appeared in the Birmingham newspaper *Aris's Gazette* on 27 April 1761:

To the Men of Sense: Wanted, for two young Ladies, whose persons are
  Amiable, straight, and free
  From natural or chance Deformity, – Pomfret two agreeable Partners for Life, Men of Integrity and Worth, between the Age of 24 and 30; if in Trade will be most agreeable. They are Ladies about the same Age, with very handsome Fortunes, and whose Characters bear the strictest Enquiry . . .

Note the creative composition of the ad, rare in this period: the quote is from the poem 'To His Friend Inclined to Marry' by John Pomfret, who was also the author of the century's best-selling and most widely read piece of verse, 'The Choice'.

The inclusion of the quote highlights the rapidly increasing literacy rates among women. The first magazine aimed solely at women, the *Ladies' Mercury*, had been launched in 1693 by John Dunton, following the success of his *Athenian Mercury*. It too dealt primarily with matters of love and marriage, specifically stipulating that it was not to be 'troubled with other questions relating to learning, religion, etc.' By 1740 it is estimated that about 40 per cent of women could read (compared to 60 per cent of men), a figure that continued to rise as the decades passed. As for being able to write, in 1754 approximately one in three brides was able to sign the marriage register, increasing to one in two by the 1840s.

The reasons for this development are manifold, ranging from increasing economic prosperity that allowed people more free time, to the invention of the penny post in 1680, which encouraged letter-writing, and the Protestant ethic centred upon reading the Bible at home. This was in addition to a general improvement in women's education. One consequence was an increase in the number of female novelists, including Fanny Burney, Maria Edgeworth and later Jane Austen. Women generally were writing and reading more, and the effect on their sex was profound and wide-ranging: 'Literacy contributed to the growth of personality, one's absorption of knowledge of self and other, and its transformations into one's own terms and purposes ...'

But who *were* the women at the vanguard of the Lonely Hearts industry? In an era when men were expected to make the first move, for a woman to place an ad was a brave step. The risk it posed to a woman's reputation was huge: 'nothing is so delicate as the reputation of a woman; it is at once the most beautiful and most brittle of all human things', as Fanny Burney put it in her best-selling novel *Evelina: Or, the History of a Young Lady's Entrance into the World* (1778). On the other hand, blatantly trumpeting one's marriageable qualities was a routine tactic among single young women: 'Belinda Portman, and her accomplishments, I'll swear, were as well advertised [at Bath], as Packwood's razor strips,' complains the future husband of the eponymous heroine in Maria Edgeworth's novel *Belinda*. Perhaps, then, to put oneself forward for consideration in the pages of a newspaper was less of a conceptual leap then than it is now. Desperate times bred desperate measures.

Of the women who advertised, the vast majority described themselves as widows. With life expectancy for men hovering at a little less than forty, it was a relatively common predicament, which in 1787 was colourfully described in an ad in *The Times* from a widow, still not thirty, who:

Women generally were reading more (1782)

very candidly acknowledges, that without a husband she cannot be happy; her evenings are spent in contemplations dictated by nature, which reason cannot obliterate, and her nights are passed in sighs and lamentations. She frequently starts in her sleep, and endeavours to embrace the beloved object of her former life, but alas! the phantom vanishes, and leaves her in a situation not to be described . . . The advertiser is sensible she has said more than many widows would say on such an occasion; but she is confident not an iota more than all widows feel at her age . . .

The remarrying widow was a stock character of eighteenth-century comedies, featuring prominently, for example, in the play *The Matrimonial Advertisement* (1777).

The Matrimonial Advertisement was written by Sarah Gardner, who began her working life as an actress. Money was always tight for her – which is why she also wrote plays – and, like many women, she was driven to extreme lengths to support herself. In 1782 she was cast in a play being performed in Dublin, but it was so poorly attended that the theatre manager claimed to be unable to pay anyone except his wife. As a result, Gardner found herself so short of funds that she embarked upon a desperate plan: she faked her own death, was given a funeral by her grief-stricken friends, then boarded a boat to the West Indies, presumably to give her creditors the slip.

Her play centres upon Mrs Holdfast, a rich young widow who has recently returned from the West Indies in search of a second husband, 'the man in the moon for aught I know . . . If he is on earth, he has been obscured from my sight hitherto'. Her independent wealth means that this 'adventurer for happiness', as Holdfast describes herself, is at liberty to prioritise love over money, making the commercial route that she takes to find herself a match a paradoxical one. She enlists the services of a hack writer, Mrs

MATRIMONY.

A Widow Lady, not yet thirty, a character without blemish, possessing a fortune of four hundred pounds per annum, and three thousand pounds well secured on a mortgage of lands in the environs of this metropolis, feels herself, notwithstanding, aukwardly situated at present: she very candidly acknowledges, that without a husband she cannot be happy; her evenings are spent in contemplations dictated by *nature*, which reason cannot obliterate; and her nights are passed in sighs and lamentations. She frequently starts in her sleep, and endeavours to embrace the beloved object of her former life, but alas! the phantom vanishes, and leaves her in a *situation not to be described*. Thus situated, she offers her hand and fortune to any Gentleman of family, who possses the following advantages—he must not exceed her own standing (thirty years;) about five feet ten inches in his stature *(an inch* will make no difference one way or the other;) perfectly in good condition; as no *diseased* Gentleman will answer her *purpose*; he must never drink above two bottles of claret, or one of port, at a sitting, and that but three times a week. His education must be liberal, and his address captivating. In company he must pay a constant attention to his spouse, and not ogle, or intrigue, by squints and looks, with pert misses, who constantly give men encouragement, by made-up leers, and manufactured sighs. He must love and cherish the woman *only* he has promised so to do in the sight of heaven. He must never set up after twelve, or rise before nine o'clock; in a word, he must be the very man he ought to be; a man *capable* and *willing* to *please a Widow*, who marries to *enjoy* the blessings of *nature*.

Any Gentleman answering the above description, and who will be serious and secret in his addresses, may be very happily situated with the Lady, who now unbesoms herself without *affectation* or *restraint*. The advertiser is sensible she has *said* more than many *widows would say* on such an occasion; but she is confident not an iota more than all *widows feel* at her age, and under similar circumstances.

§ Letters left in the Letter-box of this Paper, at the Office, Printing-house-square, Blackfriars, will be punctually attended to, and the strictest honour observed.

The Times, 25 May 1787

Epigram, to help her compose an ad, and an early version of the play contains an implicitly feminist defence of this brave step: 'And why not? . . . when a lady swerves from the general rule and makes the first advances, she is deemed indelicate. Fy! 'tis illiberal! An untainted mind is above all prejudice.' In later versions, moderated to placate London theatre managers and to appeal to audiences, this line is amended simply to 'I shall say nothing in defence of the mode.' The ad receives four replies and, after interviewing each candidate, Mrs Holdfast happily gets engaged to a kind and coura- geous Irish soldier named Carroll O'Cannon.

Mrs Holdfast describes herself in her ad as 'a young agreeable Widow with plentiful fortune; and who is very desirous of enjoying the supream felicities of the married state . . .' It sounds very much like the sort of description that appeared in real ads of the time, suggesting that Gardner had done her research. Having separated from her husband William Gardner, also an actor, in 1774 after nine years together, perhaps she had even thought of turning to Lonely Hearts ads herself. Those placed by women were distinguished by an almost total lack of personal information, an example of the 'simultaneous self-assertion and self-concealment' that was also a feature of many diaries of the time. Female advertisers tended to catalogue not their virtues, but rather their circumstances – 'I have a fortune' rather than 'I am well-educated'. Age was mentioned only by those who fall within the hallowed bracket of twenty to thirty; almost everyone else remained silent on the subject (even today, it remains far less common for a woman to state her age in an ad than a man). Those who did venture towards the personal did so only in the vaguest of terms, for instance, the ad in a Birmingham news- paper in 1784 from a 'Country young Woman, with good Health and a tolerable person, brought up in an honest and plain way' (naïve-sounding young girls like her were, after widows, those most likely to place an ad). '[I]f, from the Enquiries a Friend will privately make for her, she is so fortunate as to meet with an offer she shall like, she will soon find a Way to be introduced to the young Man.' It was a clever ploy: that way, no-one would ever know how they came to meet.

This 'Country young Woman' gives no hint of why she has chosen to track down a husband via a newspaper, but others do. 'The reason of this public application is that the Lady is almost a stranger in this metropolis,' explains an 'agreeable and accomplished Woman' in 1789. Others had got themselves into some sort of trouble. In 1777, an ad from 'a young Lady, who has lost her husband, and whose family affairs obliges her to be from her friends' contained the plea that she 'Would wish to go to France, or to Italy, or elsewhere, to travel for a few months. Must observe, that the favour of a small sum will be required, to extricate her from a little difficulty she now lies under . . .' Potential suitors were asked to write to 'E.F.' care of Mrs Boyers of Cross Street, who was the landlady of one of the many seedy lodging houses found in the back streets of Islington where women in difficulty could take refuge.

Like Eleanora, the above 'young Lady' sounds as if she has been conjured straight from the pages of a novel. The suspicion is that many ads, in particular (but not limited to) those written by women, were influenced by the popular literature of the age. Ever since Daniel Defoe's *The Family Instructor* (1715), one of the earliest novels of the sentimental genre, there had been a concern that women would get so caught up in the fantasy of such books that they would affect not only their private compositions, from diaries to letters to Lonely Hearts ads, but also their actions in real life. The seduction of Julie in Jean-Jacques Rousseau's *La nouvelle Héloïse* (1761) was blamed by some for Kitty Hunter's elopement with the (married) Earl of Pembroke. During the later decades of the century, some women displayed an almost insatiable appetite for romantic novels. In a letter to the *Lady's Monthly Museum* in 1799, a mother complained that her daughter 'reads nothing but novels . . . from morning to night . . . One week she will read in the following order: *Excessive Sensibility, Refined Delicacy, Disinterested Love, Sentimental Beauty*, etc.,' (all titles of real novels that were later to influence Austen's satirical take on the subject in *Sense and Sensibility*).

How many of those who placed a Lonely Hearts ad were simply indulging a fantasy? Were some the sort of 'boarding school damsels' characterised by Fanny Burney in the preface to *Evelina* who devoured romantic novels as fast as they could? Certainly it seems likely that the sort of men women hoped to marry was influenced by what they read. Take the 'young Gentlewoman' looking for a man 'possessed of sense, sentiment, delicacy, and humanity; in short, she wishes him to possess the endowments of the heart to an eminent degree . . . let him have stability too, and be divested of hypocrisy' (1771). She might easily have been describing Harley, the protagonist of Henry Mackenzie's novel of that same year, *The Man of Feeling*, which for the first time introduced readers to the idea of a sensitive hero in tune with his feelings.

It was Mary Wollstonecraft's view that '[Women] want a lover, and protector; and behold him kneeling before them – bravery prostate to beauty!', and many ads testify to this. Take the 'young Lady, who has lost her husband, and whose family affairs obliges her to be from her friends' looking for 'a man of fashion, honour, and sentiment, blended with good nature, and a noble spirit, such a one she would chuse for her guardian and protector . . .' (1777). While a phrase like 'a noble spirit' could easily have been lifted directly from a sentimental novel, the desire for a 'guardian and protector' is more reminiscent of another genre of literature that was popular at the time, the gothic novel. There is undoubtedly a gothic ring to the ad placed by a young lady, 'blessed with every advantage of affluence and beauty', who is 'desirous of freeing herself from the control of a cruel and capricious Guardian: she therefore informs the Public, that she would, without reluctance, throw herself into the arms of a man of spirit, who would affront danger, to rescue her from so irksome a confinement' (1781).

'The Assignation' (*The Lady's Magazine*, 1772). The fantasy of a clandestine romance was an alluring one.

The 'man of spirit' described above is just the sort of hero that was to emerge in literature, for example as Willoughby in *Sense and Sensibility* (1811), the handsome, dashing hero who comes to Marianne's rescue in the rain, literally astride a white horse. There is no doubt that there existed a degree of cross-fertilisation between private and public compositions. Thus the play *The Newspaper Wedding; or, an Advertisement for a Husband* by R. Snagg (1774) was inspired by an ad that appeared in the *Daily Advertiser* on 29 July 1772, from 'A Lady who has a real Fortune of 4000l.; and 40l. per annum, South-Sea Annuities, who about two Years ago lost a worthy Husband . . . No Objection to a Country Life'; she was looking for 'Any Person of Credit and Character, whether in or out of Trade'.

It is important to remember, however, that none of these women were the norm. Placing an ad was in essence a way of declaring one's desires in print, and thus an extraordinarily bold and even revolutionary act of defiance. For some, it must have been a profoundly empowering experience. Those looking to justify their actions were afforded further ammunition in the last decade of the century when, across the Channel in the aftermath of the French Revolution, efforts were made to remodel the courtship process better to reflect republican values. Now that the people of France had freed themselves from the rule of the King, was it not also time to free themselves from all other forms of paternalistic influence? As in England a century earlier, in the aftermath of that nation's own civil war, the result was an intellectual climate that helped Lonely Hearts ads flourish.

In 1787, one woman offered up for inspection in *The Times* her comically specific shopping list of what, in her view, constituted the ideal husband:

> . . . he must never drink above two bottles of claret, or one of port, at a sitting, and that but three times a week. His education must be liberal, and his address captivating. In

LINCOLN Flying Machine, in one Day, sets out from the Spread Eagle Inn in Gracechurch-Street, London, every Day in the Week; goes through Peterborough, Bourne, Falkingham, Sleaford, and Lincoln; gets to Hull and Barton Humber in a Day and a Half; returns every Day to the above Spread Eagle Inn, in London. The above Carriages will carry Parcels at the most reasonable Rates. Performed by Alexander Bell, Wm. Dymoke, of London; Wm. Biger, Wm. Boulton, of Peterborough; Ishmael Goodhand, of Lincoln, and Co.

BOARD and Lodging is wanted for a Widow Gentlewoman, within a few Miles of London, has no Objection to going where there are Boarders; a Farm House, or where there are several in Family, will be most agreeable; the Advertiser will find her own Tea, Linnen, and Washing; to prevent Trouble, &c. per Ann. only will be given. Please to direct to E. N. at the London-Bridge Coffee-House, mentioning the Situation and Family, which if approved shall be speedily answered.

WANTED, Board and Lodging in the Country, for a Lady and her Maid, not more than four Miles distant from the Royal Exchange, in an agreeable Family, where there is a chearful Female Companion or two, and the better Church the more agreeable. Direct to A. B. (mentioning Particulars) at the Chapter Coffee-House, St. Paul's Church Yard.

ANY Person disposed to advance 100l. may have an Opportunity of entering into Partnership, or on Loan, on advantageous and secure Terms. A Line left at the Nag's Head, James-Street, Covent-Garden, shall have due Attention paid.

FROM 30l. to 60l. will be given to any Lady or Gentleman who has it in their Power to procure a little or preferable Tidesman's Place in the Custom-House for a sober Man, or in any other Publick Office under the Government, where not much Education is required. A Line directed for J. D. at Mr. Atkinson's, Baker, the Top of Rupert-Street, near St. Ann's Church, Soho, shall be duly answered. Honour and Secrecy may be depended upon.

MARRIAGE, a serious Proposal. A Lady who has a real Fortune of 2000l. and 30l. per Annum, South-Sea Annuities, who about two Years ago lost a worthy Husband, is again disposed to enter into the Married State, if she can find a Man to her Mind. She is on Terms of the strictest Honour, and expects honourable and candid Treatment; and that the most profound Secrecy will be observed. Any Person of Credit and Character, whether in or out of Trade, may address a Line to H. S. to be left at Mr. Riley's, Bookseller, in Curzon Street. Any Letter not properly answered shall be kept. No Objection to a Country Life.

WANTED, a sober diligent Person to take the Management of a School about 66 Miles from London; such Person must write a good Hand, and understand Arithmetick very well; also he must be very well qualified to teach Drawing, both in School and out in the Town, as Occasion may require. Letters directed for Mr. Weddington, Teacher of

Daily Advertiser, 29 July 1772

company he must pay a constant attention to his spouse, and not ogle, or intrigue, by squints and looks, with pert misses, who constantly give men encouragement, by made-up leers, and manufactured sight. He must love and cherish the women only he has promised so to do in the sight of heaven. He must never get up after twelve, or rise before nine o'clock; in a word, he must be the very man he ought to be . . .

Most were more prosaic and practical in their demands. In *Aris's Gazette* in 1784, a woman from the Midlands sought out 'any sober, good-tempered, well-looking young Man, between Twenty and Thirty, who is settled in a good Trade in Birmingham, or that Neighbourhood . . . N.B. My Father says Trade is better than the Farming Business.' Implicitly this ad is all about money. As *Pride and Prejudice*'s Elizabeth Bennet was to muse, '. . . what is the difference in matrimonial affairs, between the mercenary and the prudent motive? Where does discretion end, and avarice begin?'

Some, however, were so desperate that they were ready to race to the altar with any man who would have them. Widows in particular frequently carried pathetically low expectations about the sort of man they might hope to attract: 'she is not so vain as to expect a gentleman,' clarified one in the *Public Advertiser* in 1768, despite the fact that she was still young – not yet twenty-six – and had an annual income of 24l. a year, in addition to 500l. in savings. In 1776, a young widow in 'distressed circumstances' by the name of Sylvia offered herself up to any 'single gentleman of honour and fortune' who might want to 'engage her as the superintendant of his family'. 'Whoever shall think fit to make her the object of his choice,' she continued, 'may depend on the most affectionate and grateful returns.' It is the fundamentally passive tone of Sylvia's appeal that breaks one's heart. But then Sylvia is clearly a realist, under no illusions that a wife's role is basically that of the family 'superintendant'; her ad, like many women's, is almost entirely geared towards the male fantasy, with little or no expression of her own sense of self. For many, as Mary Wollstonecraft was convinced, marriage was simply a form of socially sanctioned prostitution.

There is no doubt that at least some of the bodies on offer in the personal columns were literally selling sex. While prostitutes would not have had the means or the need to place an ad, the same cannot be said of courtesans. Kitty Fisher once placed an ad in the *Public Advertiser* to clear her name, and while Kitty herself did not need to pursue such a route to drum up custom (she was so successful that she was once said to have eaten a fifty-pound note in a sandwich), there were other, less well-known courtesans, whose names have now been lost to us, who would. The 19 December 1768 edition of the *Gazetteer* carried the following ad:

> A Lady, whose accomplishments hath acquired the esteem of the *beau monde*, having lately lost a secret friend, is desirous of putting herself under the protection of any person of rank and fortune. Person agreeable; disposition happy; can suit herself either to the sprightly levity of the gay, or the more sedate turn of the grave and wise. Though brought up in the *bon ton*, her reason is not impaired. Her real situation is an entire secret to her acquaintance, which she hopes will apologize for this address. A line, post paid, for N.N. at the Cecil-street Coffee-house, Strand, till called for, shall be attended to.

This advertiser professes herself happy to tailor herself to the whims of her buyer, almost as if she is a custom-made dress.

Then there are those who are perhaps not exactly courtesans, but who are not entirely respectable either. The clue is when marriage goes unmentioned; instead, it is the rather more vague 'protection' that is sought. Such is the ad placed in 1782 by 'A Lady, with a genteel Education, [who] should think herself highly honoured to be protected by an elderly Gentleman of generosity, whose heart may be inclined to render her happy . . . No relations or acquaintances to intrude, nor any objection to retirement.' Others simply fancy a jaunt abroad: in 1790 letters were to be left for 'C.S.' at Mr Williams's, a shoemaker's on Oxford Street, from 'any Single Gentleman who may have occasion to make a Tour into France, and who may perhaps think the company of a Lady, certainly not disagreeable, an addition to his Tour'.

Women were implicated not only in writing Lonely Hearts ads, but even more so in reading them. Towards the end of the century, wealthier women in particular had more leisure time than ever before. As Vic Gatrell explains it: 'It may be overstating it to say that English cultural life was being "feminized" in these decades; yet it is true that cultivated middle-class women were joining their better-born sisters as cultural producers and consumers in the second half of the eighteenth century, and as opinion-makers too.'

For some women, browsing the Lonely Hearts ads held a special, almost perverse appeal, particularly when it came to ads like Eleonora's. 'There is a sort of luxury in giving way to the feelings!' admitted Elizabeth Fry in her diary. 'I love to feel for the sorrows of others, to pour wine and oil into the wounds of the afflicted; there is a luxury in feeling the heart glow, whether it be with joy or sorrow . . .' This was also true of reading novels, where concerns surrounded the prospect of women becoming sexually aroused. In Mary Wollstonecraft's autobiographical novel *Mary* (1788) the heroine's voracious reading is described as resulting in 'the development of the passions' – the pleasure she finds in novels acting as the 'most delightful substitutes for bodily dissipations'. Reading a Lonely Hearts ad can indeed function as a way of indulging a sexual fantasy: What specimen of a man is the advertiser? What wonderful adventures might result from a *rendezvous*? No doubt some newspaper proprietors, seeing how well romantic fiction sold, sought to tap into the same market, taking advantage of an entirely new customer base – women – whom they ignored at their peril.

Occasionally some women were even moved to put pen to paper and reply to an ad. There were certainly worse ways to spend a rainy afternoon. Giggling with a friend, why not scribble a missive to a thirty-two-year-old gentleman looking for an affectionate lady with £500 a year? Or, more likely, why not shut oneself away in one's closet to write to someone who might – just might – be the man of one's dreams? A closet, which in this sense constituted a small room adjoining the bedroom, was a defining feature of the typical Georgian mansion and, as Samuel Richardson put it in his novel *Pamela* (1740), a woman 'makes her closet her paradise'. It was a place for reading, the very privacy of which 'opens up possibilities for independence of mind, freedom of thought, and deviance from the norm'. It was also a place for writing, in particular letter-writing (Pamela herself used her closet to scribble endless missives), an act of self-expression that has been linked by some to eighteenth-century women's increasingly powerful sense of selfhood. And sometimes it was a place simply to be alone, a potentially subversive state of affairs in itself: according to Mary Wollstonecraft, 'Solitude and reflection are necessary to give to wishes the force of passions, and to enable the imagination to enlarge the object, and make it more desirable.' After all, a little bit of delightful day-dreaming has the potential to lead to all kinds of shenanigans, even perhaps to the private indulgence of the sexual fantasies provoked by the very Lonely Hearts ads that had appeared in that morning's *Times*.

'[A]lways of an active and enterprising turn': this is how Maria Hunter, in her play *Fitzroy* (1792), described the sort of women who replied to Lonely Hearts ads. Male playwrights, however, tended to be rather less complimentary. In *Indiscretion* by Prince Hoare (1800) such women are variously characterised as 'some starch old maiden, wound up for a parley ... Or some lady's waiting maid, full of all the delicacies of speech, studied from her mistress's toilette ... Or some artful courtesan, who will persuade him, she is the distant branch of some very respectable but decayed family ...' For respectable women, the sheer logistics of depositing a written reply to an ad at the appointed location was a conundrum in itself. Coffee-houses were

'Mr. B. finds Pamela writing' by Joseph Highmore (1692–1780)

a predominantly male affair, so a woman would have been unable to enter one without making herself highly conspicuous; the only option would have been to send a trusted male on her behalf – and this was one reason why, from the 1780s, coffee-houses were gradually superseded by shops, newspaper offices or libraries as the principal point of contact.

Beauty in Search of Knowledge (1782)

The anonymous print entitled *Beauty in Search of Knowledge* (1782) depicts a woman sauntering past a circulating library, and it is normally assumed that her intentions are of the high-minded literary sort. She may, however, have been dropping off a reply to an ad, like the one that appeared in 1781 from 'A Person not quite forty years of age, of a genteel address and affable disposition, who has acquired, by his own identity, between sixty and seventy pounds a year, and can get, by a few hours attendance in a morning, a hundred pounds per annum, intends to quit trade and retire to a pleasant spot near Town'; he was hoping to meet 'an agreeable Gentlewoman, suitable to his own age, possest [*sic*] of about fifteen hundred pounds, or an yearly income of seventy pounds . . . who is not too fond of the present mode of dress, and can conform to a dome-stick way of life'. Letters were to be left at Mr Milne's Circulating Library at 202 High Holborn. Look closely at the print, and the woman in question does seem to have something of a glint in her eye. For her sort, a dalliance in the world of Lonely Hearts ads would have provided a welcome distraction from the boredom of everyday life at the upper end of the social scale. It was an attempt at an inner life, which, in an age when aristocrats seemed only to appear in public in crowds ('swarming' was how Louis Simond described it), was hard to come by. It established them as somehow different, or 'singular' in the parlance of the day. It was these women who were the ones with time to read the newspaper, compose a reply, deliver it (or ask their maid or coach-driver to), and endlessly discuss the hilarious results over tea the next morning with their friends.

But, in general, women replied to Lonely Hearts ads out of need. In 1776, an ad appeared in the *Public Advertiser* from a fifty-some-thing Member of Parliament who 'lives in great splendour, and from whom a considerable Estate must pass if he dies without issue', who 'hath no objection to marry any Widow or single Lady, provided the party be of genteel birth, polite manners, and five, six, seven, or eight Months gone in her Pregnancy . . .' Similarly, in 1788 the *Hibernian Telegraph* printed an extraordinary offer from a 'gentleman advanced in years, who is possessed of a considerable fortune, the apparent heir to which (a graceless nephew) has treated him in a manner unpardonable . . .' In retaliation at the way his nephew had behaved, he announced that he 'would be glad to enter into the connubial state with a healthy *pregnant* widow, of a reputation *unsullied*, however contracted her sphere of life be'. For some woman in trouble somewhere, such an ad must have seemed heaven-sent. It is also just one example of the way that Lonely Hearts ads have a knack of defying historical clichés. Getting pregnant out of wedlock did not necessarily have to be the total disaster that convention might portray it to be. Though opportunities to turn the situation to one's advantage were exceptionally rare, they did exist. And one place to look for them was in the personal column of a newspaper.

Chapter Five

Enterprizing Enamoratos

IF YOU WERE to wander the streets of Windsor any afternoon during the 1790s, you would have come across a very strange sight. Tottering along, a loaf of bread in one hand and a whole live fish in the other, a long blue cloak swishing behind him, would have been fifth baronet Sir John Dineley. He was born in Herefordshire in about 1729, but when he was fourteen his father was murdered by his uncle over an inheritance dispute. So, while the title passed to him, he received no money or property and ended up practically destitute. Fortunately, he was soon appointed a Poor Knight of Windsor, which meant that he received a pension and accommodation in the grounds of Windsor Castle.

Every morning for the rest of his life Sir John stepped out of his two-bedroom cottage in the grounds of Windsor Castle's Lower Ward, locked the door behind him (he had not entertained any visitors in decades) and wandered out through the castle gate and into the streets of Windsor to stock up on provisions. He always made sure he was back at the castle in time to attend the daily church service at St George's Chapel, which by the terms of the statutes of the Order of the Garter, Poor Knights were duty-bound to attend. For special occasions — for example, if royalty came to town and he knew there would be women around — Sir John changed into a more lavish outfit of an embroidered coat, a flowery waistcoat and velvet pantaloons that almost (but not quite) covered up the dirty silk stockings he wore at all times. He would also add a little powder to his wig.

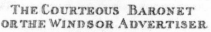

One of Sir John Dineley's leaflets (1799)

When Sir John came across a woman in the street, he would bow to her, hand her a leaflet addressed 'To the fair ladies of Great Britain, old or young' and stalk away without so much as a word of introduction. This went on throughout the 1790s, but when it failed to produce a prospective wife, he moved on to placing ads in *The Times*, the *Morning Advertiser* and various local papers. Here is one from the 21 August 1802 edition of the *Ipswich Journal*:

> To the angelic fair of the true English breed. Worthy notice. Sir John Dineley, of Windsor Castle, recommends himself and his ample fortune to any angelic beauty of a good breed, fit to become and willing to be the mother of a noble heir, and keep up the name of an ancient family ennobled by deeds of arms and ancestral renown. Ladies at a certain period of life need not apply. Fortune favours the bold . . .

He put similar ads in the London newspapers every time he went up to town, which he did two or three times a year in order to trawl for a wife on Drury Lane and at Vauxhall Gardens, both well-known hunting grounds. He also tried printing his own pamphlets, including one entitled *Method to Get Husbands*, which featured a six-page-long poem detailing the sort of women he thought might answer his ad: 'the sickly Damsel, who has long pined in secret . . . The woe begone Widow, whose weeds are an almost insupportable load . . . And the sweet blooming Miss of Sixteen, to whom the trammels of a boarding-school are quite intolerable . . .' Still not a single prospective Mrs Dineley introduced herself to him. Then, one morning in November 1809, Sir John did not come to church. Some locals went to his house, broke down his front door and found him lying ill in bed, surrounded by printing materials. He died a few days later.

Sir John received an enormous amount of publicity in both the local and national press over the course of the fifteen years during which he so actively, albeit fruitlessly, pursued his search for a wife.

There was quite the audience for it: by the 1790s more than half a million morning newspapers were sold every day in London alone, and the saga proved to be a source of great amusement. Even the baronet was aware that some mocked his efforts, 'that some few, prejudiced by etiquette, may smile at his mode of address; let them laugh . . .' he defiantly declared. On this subject, he was correct: public perception of Lonely Hearts ads in later Georgian Britain was, in essence, that they were all one big scam.

'Advertisements of this Kind are too often inserted for idle Amusement,' claimed one advertiser in 1772, and he was not unusual in his view. Many warned against those who replied out of 'curiosity' or for a 'diversion', and in 1789 Prussian traveller Johann D'Archenholz commented: 'Some people insert ads of this kind merely from pastime. Under different signatures they pretend to want husbands and wives, and manage interviews between the persons who answer them; this often gives occasion to the most comical scenes.' It is true that some ads do raise suspicions, such as those that demand real names and addresses. It could even be that every single ad quoted thus far is a complete fabrication. There is simply no way of knowing for sure. On the other hand, it was not until thirty or so years later that reports of definite hoaxes began to appear in the newspapers. This does not mean that they did not happen previously, but it does suggest that they were by no means commonplace.

Furthermore, no Lonely Hearts ad is ever completely genuine. It is an industry built upon making false or exaggerated claims: the advertiser's 'virtues [are] like those of a quack medicine – not to be found out of the advertisement'. We all misrepresent ourselves to an extent during the courtship process; only a fool admits too early on that they have been sacked from three jobs or have fat thighs. Instead, we wear a mask in order to maintain our private image, and a Lonely Hearts ad allows us to remould our identity in whatever way we please.

Some Regency readers believed that, if not a scam, all those who advertised were at the very least in search of sex. This may well have been true, in part: sex, in particular sexual fantasy, has always been part of the appeal of Lonely Hearts ads. Take 'R.R.', who in 1777 declared to readers of the *Daily Advertiser* that it was not a wife he was after, but rather a mistress: 'Any lady, agreeable and accomplished, who can disspence with age &c for the sake of a good estate, and a coach and six, may assuredly find a friend who has it fully in his power to accomplice such a matter to her very wish, provided such a lady will do the proposer a particular favour, which may be in her power consistent with the *nicest honour*.' In the 1770s, phrases like 'Would prefer a connection without a tie' or 'matrimony is not his view' began to appear with increasing frequency. Ads of this sort were later noted by, among others, the Romantic poet Robert Southey:

> Sometimes a gentleman advertises for a wife, sometimes a lady for a husband. Intrigues are carried on in them, and assignations made between A.B. and C.D. . . . At this very time a gent is offering a thousand pounds to any lady who can serve him in a delicate affair; a lady has answered him, they have had their meeting, she does not suit his purpose, and he renews the offer of his enormous bribe, which in all probability is meant as the price of some enormous villainy.

In 1779, an ad appeared in the *Morning Post* from a 'Gentleman of Fortune' who, conversely, sought to dispose of his mistress. Because 'Family reasons oblige to drop a connection which has for some time subsisted between him and an agreeable young Lady', he was willing to 'give a considerable sum of Money with her to any Gentleman, or person in genteel Business, who has good sense and resolution to despise the censures of the World, and will enter with her into the Holy state of Matrimony . . .' Ads like this contributed to the perception that the personal columns were a hotbed of sexual intrigue.

The most common assumption, however, was that any man bold enough to advertise for a wife in a newspaper was only after one thing: money. This was a risk even for those who entered the courtship arena via a more conventional route, with the *Matrimonial Magazine* warning of 'those dangerous Adventurers, whose Designs being more against the Purses than Person of the Ladies, have obtained them the name of *Fortune-hunters*: A Set of enterprizing Enamoratos, who constantly attend at Bath, Bristol, Southampton, and the other Watering-Places of the Kingdom, to shew their Affection for rich Heiresses, or administer Comfort to wealthy Widows.' But the risk was multiplied many times over by the anonymity offered by the personal columns. In 1775, 'A Gentleman of Honour and Property' announced to readers of the *Morning Post* that he wished to sell off his ward, though he phrased it a little more delicately than this: 'having in his disposal at present a young Lady of good Family, with a fortune of Sixty Thousand Pounds, on her Marriage with his approbation, [he] would be very happy to treat with a Man of Fashion and Family, who may think it worth his while to give the Advertiser a Gratuity of Five thousand pounds on the day of Marriage'. Nothing and nobody was exempt from the drive to make money. This was a society where it had now become acceptable to buy and sell women in public, as though they were hats or horses. And while this was not necessarily a new tactic, it was an increasingly blatant one.

D'Archenholz offered up some advice on how to spot a fortune-hunter: 'If they are not able to enumerate a catalogue of their personal accomplishments, they are sure to boast of their good sense, their excellent character; and, in one word, of their inclination to consult, on all occasions, the happiness of their future wives.' Some advertisers were so dubious-sounding that it is hard to believe anyone actually fell for them. There was, for example, the 'Gentleman' in 1782 who sought 'a Lady possessing an ample fortune at her own disposal, as he cannot boast of acquired parts, yet he flatters himself, nature has done him justice in a great degree, no other accomplishment will be thought necessary in the Lady. – The advertiser [is] anxious that the consummation should take place on or before the 10th day March next . . .' Others were more concise: 'Any Lady of fortune' was the single requirement in one decidedly suspicious ad of 1790.

D'Archenholz further warned against female fortune-hunters. These 'Women of the town' set their traps in such a way that:

> Young men bred in the country, and others without experience, often fall into the snare. On an interview, they find these bewitching creatures, who appear as mild and gentle as innocence itself, know how to affect their compassion, by a touching recital of the persecutions of their relations or guardians; and never fail to make it appear clearly, that it would be the easiest thing in the world to get possession of their fortune. This story has the proper effect; the simpleton believes every thing, and never finds, till too late, that he has been grossly imposed upon.

D'Archenholz may or may not have been right. It is possible that an ad like that of 'Eleanora' in 1788, in which she complained of 'the tyranny of her family on the one hand, and the impositions of lawyers on the other', was merely a ruse by some cunning courtesan to drum up business. It is more likely, however, that D'Archenholz was indulging his own uninformed assumptions – assumptions that reflected a profound anxiety surrounding women's slowly but steadily increasing empowerment, both sexual and otherwise.

The perception that con-artists and fortune-hunters lurked between every line of the personal columns meant that many advertisers were increasingly assertive in their attempts to pre-empt criticism from the moral majority. Take the self-righteous 'Young Gentleman of good family and connexions' who in 1778 was about to move abroad and 'would be glad of a partner for life; he is extremely sorry that his short stay in London has made it necessary to have recourse to an expedient he has always detested; his motives therefore are very different from those which tempt most people to make use of so uncommon a method of attracting the Ladies attention . . .' Many acknowledged the risk that women faced: 'any Lady may answer this without fear or intimidation' was the reassurance given in *The Times* in 1795. Some told readers that nobody would be required to give their real name until an interview had taken place; others offered multiple references. It was also not uncommon to resort to threats against anyone who sought to trifle with the advertiser: 'It is hoped that none out of wanton curiosity will apply to this address, as they may have reason to repent their conduct' (1782). With so many seeking to deter the undesirables, it is clear that these ads had a considerable image problem.

In 1788, an ad appeared in *The Times* allegedly placed by 'A Polite Citizen about thirty years of age, and who has been four years in business, finding that trade neither agrees with the sentiments of his mind, nor the constitution of his purse, thinks it absolutely requisite to try the effects of matrimony, in order to save his credit in the mercantile worlds, and preserve his honour in the fashionable circle.' It was requested that letters be left at Tom's Coffee House, ideally 'as soon as possible, as the docket will probably be struck before Christmas, and then the ladies will for ever lose this honourable opportunity, the advertiser, if he escapes the drop, meaning to retire under the statute of uncertified bankrupts, to the King's Bench for life'. The assumption that the personal columns were awash with fortune-hunters, both male and female, had become so widespread that it was now the target of mainstream humour.

ADVERTISEMENT EXTRAORDINARY.

MATRIMONY.

A polite Citizen about thirty years of age, and who has been four years in business, finding that trade neither agrees with the sentiments of his mind, nor the constitution of his purse, thinks it absolutely requisite to try the effects of matrimony, in order to save his credit in the mercantile world, and preserve his honour in the fashionable circle.

An early inclination having fostered the parade at St. James's, in preference to the 'Change in Cornhill, he intended himself for a soldier instead of a merchant : but the family having made a fortune in commerce, his father sentenced him to the compting house in place of the guard room, and he was obliged to guide a pen, instead of brandishing a sword.

A country house, a hunting lodge, two whiskeys, a curricle and a phæton, with an expensive mistress, city dice, and Westminster faro, obliged him for the credit of his character, to call in the assistance of respectable names, without either their authority or their knowledge, to keep up the honour of a merchant : but the late failures having put monied men upon their guard against all manufactured bills, those illegally borrowed acceptances and indorsements verge towards the day of retribution, without the means of preventing detection, by discharging the bills when presented.

Any Lady of fortune, therefore, who wishes to join herself in matrimony with a *Fashionable Merchant* high in credit, respectable on 'Change, and admired in the polite circle, has now a very fair opportunity of escaping the cruelty of careful parents, the horrors of perpetual virginity, or the odious epithet of old maid, for it is totally indifferent to the advertiser, whether he prevents ruin to himself by a marriage with beauty and innocence—age and ugliness—deformity and vice—pride and incontinence—arrogance and wit—meretriciousness and prudery—or all that is admirable—or all that is to be despised, so that the Lady has a sufficiency of cash to extricate him from his present difficulties.

The Lady may rest assured, that the advertiser will do all in his power to make a proper return for the favour conferred on him, and as no good qualifications are required, nor any time of life objectionable, there is little doubt but the married state will prove at least *fashionably happy*.

The more advanced in years, the more respectable will be the Lady who offers, and all proper decency shall be kept up during the first month, vulgarly called the honey moon—and this promise is most solemnly made, and will be punctually adhered to—that the Lady after the hour of consummation, may *command* her husband (if the fortune be properly secured in his favour) to *any distance* from her converse and person.

An answer to *Gig Curricle, Esq.* at Tom's Coffee House, is earnestly requested as soon as possible, as the docket will probably be struck before Christmas, and then the ladies will for ever lose this honourable opportunity, the advertiser, if he escapes the drop, meaning to retire under the statute of uncertified bankrupts, to the King's Bench for life.

The Times, 18 November 1788

The joke rapidly gained momentum. Take a satirical print drawn
in 1792 by Richard Newton at the unlikely age of fifteen:

From *Advertisement Illustrated* by Richard Newton (1792)

That same year, *Fitzroy* by Maria Hunter hit the London stage,
further perpetuating the perception that fortune-hunters routinely
stalked the personal columns looking for prey. The play features a
Mr Maddison who, having recently lost a lot of money at the poker
table, 'was now reduced to his last stake . . . he tried various means
to counteract the malignity of the Goddess Fortune: among the rest
he had published a matrimonial advertisement'.

Similar ground had been covered by *Love in the City* by Isaac Bickerstaffe (1767), a comic opera whose main claim to fame is that it features the world's first (and hopefully last) musical Lonely Hearts ad, and by *The Matrimonial Advertisement* by Sarah Gardner (1777). But it was in the 1790s that Lonely Hearts ads really entered the mainstream cultural consciousness, not only in *Fitzroy*, but in a number of other plays on the same subject, including *Fortune's Fool* by the popular dramatist Frederick Reynolds (1796). By then Lonely Hearts ads had become sufficiently surrounded by a generally accepted set of assumptions – in particular, that any man who advertised was only after money – that it was pretty certain that the average London theatregoer would get the joke. It was, after all, a distinctive characteristic of the later Georgian era that everyone laughed at everything that in any way dared to veer from the strictures of convention.

These plays also helped channel the general debate about marriage that was conducted in the aftermath of the American and French Revolutions. Loud cries for improved women's rights were being heard all over Europe, focusing particularly on the fight for some semblance of equality between husband and wife. Furthermore, the matter of the nation's sexual morality was at the top of the agenda: London's population of prostitutes was said to have hit an all-time high of 50,000. Many people demanded full-scale moral reform. Add to this the outbreak of war with France in 1793, and the result was a widespread sense of malaise, in spite of Britain's growing prosperity. 'We are threatened with Invasion; we are loaded with Debts and Taxes; we are divided and weakened by Parties; we are sunk in Doom and Despair,' according to the writer and moralist John Bowdler. The ongoing fear that France might invade at any moment led to a general jitteriness that was channelled into a host of other worries about more minor, tangible aspects of modern life – worries that frequently found cultural expression in one form or another.

'[Matrimonial] advertisements fill a large part of the paper,' according to Robert Southey in 1807. 'A selection of these advertisements would form a curious book, and exhibit much of the state of England . . .' Indeed. As the ever-present determination to keep a Lonely Hearts ad a secret intensified, by the turn of the century almost all concluded with some sort of reassurance. An ad was inserted in *The Times* by 'The Friend of a Gentleman (a Bachelor), about 26 . . . without [the friend's] knowledge, by which means he hopes to introduce a Lady to his wishes, and prevent the possibility of prejudice on his part by this too common channel of information'. This was despite the deeply paradoxical nature of requests of this sort: 'A secret in the newspaper, which you wouldn't have known for the world!' The ads challenge the theory put forward by some historians that it was in the eighteenth century that Britain's public and private spheres irrevocably separated from one another. There is no place more public than a newspaper, no matter more personal than marriage, yet in the small-ads section of many an eighteenth-century newspaper the two were often intimately intertwined.

The obsession with secrecy was largely a response to an increased and pervasive fear of fraud that typified the times. 'We must acknowledge that there never was an age or a country so favourable to the success of imposture, as this very age and this very England,' to quote Robert Southey again. '[I]mposture' by means of a Lonely Hearts ad was the principal plot device of many a well-attended Drury Lane farce. In *Winning a Husband* by George Macfarren (1819), a mischievous maid sets up a series of meetings with Sir Roderick Strangeways in response to his newspaper ad, each of which she attends disguised as a different stock comic character. Increased social mobility as a result of the Industrial Revolution meant that an individual's identity was more fluid than ever before. If plays like *Winning a Husband* functioned as a 'public negotiation of the meanings of marriage', then one of these meanings was that those brave or foolish enough to take their quest for a spouse into the public domain left themselves open to the possibility of identity fraud. And so it was that the city laughed at precisely what it feared.

Wanted: a wife by W.T. Moncrieff (1819) centres upon a case of genuine mistaken identity: an ad is placed looking for a wife, another one for a servant, and the inevitable mix-up results in all kinds of farcical shenanigans. The inbuilt potential for different social classes to interact made Lonely Hearts ads a perfect subject for romantic comedies. This was also, however, another reason why they scared people. By allowing all levels of society to mix and match in the pages of the paper, Lonely Hearts ads encouraged class transgression – which, following the American and French Revolutions, had become a very real source of concern.

THE ADVERTISEMENT FOR A WIFE.

Advertisement for a Wife by Thomas Rowlandson (1821). How is the advertiser, Rowlandson's satirical creation Dr Syntax, to know that any of the crowd of seemingly desperate women who have replied to his ad really are who they say they are?

The following year, *X.Y.Z.* by George Colman (1820) was offered up to London audiences. The play opens with Neddy Bray placing an ad in the *Morning Post*: '[E]ver since I was eighteen, I have been pining and sighing after the blessings of the married state; but some how or other I could never muster courage to pop the question to any lady in my life.' Bray is careful to keep his identity a secret when he places his ad: 'I took it to the office, with the money, myself. I went in a Brutus wig, and a barouche great coat; so I defy 'em to tell whether I was a fine gentleman, or a hackney coachman . . .' The same day, however, an ad is also placed in rival newspaper the *Morning Herald* for an actress in an American theatre. Confusion ensues, and the play concludes with the moral that 'the less we trust to anonymous advertisements, in future, the better'. It was a moral that accurately captured public perceptions. Whether it was fair or not is another matter.

There is no doubt that at least some Lonely Hearts ads were just as suspect as playwrights, caricaturists, commentators and indeed some of the advertisers themselves made out. And from the 1820s onwards, cautionary tales regularly began to make it into the newspapers for the first time. One in the *Morning Chronicle* in 1825 described how a group of 'young men who estimated well the force of vanity in their own sex, lately agreed on an experiment'. They inserted an ad in a number of daily newspapers, which resulted in more than fifty replies. They then inserted a second ad,

> stating that the answer of A.B. (or C.X. or whatever other title the wooer chose) had been received, and in order to secure a personal interview he was desired to be at Drury-lane Theatre, in the boxes, on a certain night, in a certain dress, and at the end of the play to stand up and apply a quizzing glass to his right eye. At the time appointed, the whole fifty were there; all started forward – all raised their quizzing glass, but almost at the same moment each saw himself multiplied fifty-fold;

they became sensible of the hoax, and suddenly disappeared, and gave up at once their hopes of enjoying beauty and a fortune.

While japes of this sort were not nearly as common as they were to become by the end of the century, there is no doubt that they did happen.

There is, however, no evidence of actual criminal fraud. This does not mean that it did not happen (there will always be crooks and swindlers wherever there is money to be made), but rather that it did not come to court. Until the beginning of George IV's reign most people were not yet aware of the potential for criminal gain that Lonely Hearts ads offered, and as a consequence far fewer ads actually were fraudulent than cynics assumed. But the perception that the personal columns were entirely peopled by eccentrics, jokers and fraudsters was not based on fact. Rather, it was an outlet for a range of other anxieties. Along with so much else in industrialising Britain, the rules of courtship and marriage were shifting. The increasingly public nature of modern life meant that even the search for love was no longer a uniformly private affair.

Yet the personal columns survived, not least because they continued to provide a genuine service. One fellow in 1825 testified to the fact that he had 'heard many happy unions have been effected by this mode . . .' This had to be so, otherwise the business of advertising for love would not have continued to flourish as it did.

Newspapers did not have the monopoly. Britain's first marriage agency had announced itself to the world in the *Daily Advertiser* back in 1758. It claimed to have been founded by 'A Person of character, candour and honour, who has an entire knowledge of the World, and has great Intimacy with both Sexes among the Nobility, Gentry and Persons of Credit and Reputation'. He was never heard from again, sadly, but others soon picked up the mantle. In 1775, hundreds of

A Ball at Scarborough by James Green (1813)

Plymouth Playhouse by Thomas Rowlandson (1818)

A variety of social gatherings existed in order to facilitate the
matrimonial process. But when these failed to throw up an eligible
suitor, there were alternative avenues . . .

handbills were distributed on the streets of London to promote a marriage agency based at 2 Dover Street near St James's (it also advertised in a couple of newspapers). It was aimed at men who 'have neither Time nor Temper for the tedious Forms of Courtship' and at women who 'tied down by Custom to be passive, cannot be first Movers in a Point so delicate'. Applicants were asked to write a description of themselves, 'not only the Situation in Life, but the Age, Constitution, and Religion', and to call between 11 a.m. and 4 p.m. or 7 p.m. and 10 p.m. any day except Sundays, when they would then be asked to hand over the not inconsiderable sum of five guineas. The proprietors rather undermined their repeated assertions of respectability, however, by proclaiming that they were also in the business of lending sums of money from £500 upwards, 'upon the shortest Notice'.

The following year, a reader calling himself 'Lothario' wrote in to *Town and Country* to complain about the Dover Street agency. *Town and Country* was a monthly magazine founded in 1769 and mostly devoted to scandal, so this sort of story was right up their street. 'Lothario' described how he had paid his five guineas, been informed that the agency had found him a perfect match and that the lady in question had agreed to meet him in Gray's Inn Gardens, stipulating only that he bring with him a large nosegay tied in a blue ribbon to present to her. This he did, but it then transpired that she was actually an old acquaintance of his, much to his irritation. It was a chain of events that was forcefully rebutted in an ad in the *Morning Post* from the agency's proprietors. They protested at 'a very illiberal, unjust Assertion, viz., that any new Plan or Scheme that is offered to the Public is founded upon Imposition'.

This public spat served to confirm the widely held opinion that the entire matrimonial business – whether ads or agencies – was just another form of quackery. Among the guests present at a lavish masked ball held at Carlisle House in Soho Square in 1776 was one who came dressed as a marriage broker. Throughout the evening he handed out business cards printed with the following: 'The Marriage Broker accommodates ladies and gentlemen with every-thing in the matrimonial way which their hearts can wish for (virtue and money only excepted), and that at first sight of the parties, having fitted up a variety of very commodious apartments, suited either for *ante*-matrimonial experiments or *post*-nuptial consumma-tion . . .' The intention was to make the assembled guests laugh, and no doubt he succeeded: the ethically dubious marriage broker had by this time become a stock comic character that society loved to mock.

Other attempts to make money out of marriage included the Imprejudicate Nuptial Society in 1795 ('in the common way men first fall in love, and then disgracefully retreat, if there is not money enough; but here the circumstances are first known, and nothing to prevent sincere love afterwards'), the New Matrimonial Plan in 1820 (the selling point of which was that all subscribers were categorised from first-class to fifth-class in order to prevent any sort of class transgression) and the Imperial Matrimonial Association in 1825 (a membership club for single men and women with its own suite of rooms in central London which were stocked with magazines and hosted twice-weekly concerts).

None of these enterprises lasted long, however, partly due to the public's suspicion. In the play *The New Marriage Act; or, Look before you leap* (1822) by Archibald Maclaren, Shuffle (who, it is later revealed, is not only a crook, but already married) describes how he recently married a 'beautiful young lady' whom he came across when he 'saw her name at the match-making office, where, for half-a-crown, you may look over a list of the fairest faces and heaviest purses'. It was a line that the audience would have enjoyed, for it played on the public perception that this was exactly the kind of thing that always went on at matchmaking offices.

This was a specifically British attitude. On the Continent, and in particular in France, marriage brokers were well accepted, and had been for many years. One of the best-known was Monsieur Brunet, whose ads appeared in (among other places) *Galignani's*, an English newspaper published in Paris. One typical edition had up for grabs:

1. A young lady, aged 22, of a most agreeable countenance, having 300,000 francs;
2. One, aged 20, having 120,000 francs;
3. One, having 150,000 francs;
4. One, having 175,000 francs.

Also, three widows, aged 25, 30, and 35, having 10,000, 15,000 and 20,000 francs of yearly income.

Yet advertising for love continued to thrive. Before long, even Lord Byron had become aware that it was an option, confiding in Lady Melbourne that 'I admired your niece, but she is engaged . . . – Besides she deserves a better heart than mine – What shall I do – shall I *advertise?*' The implication is that there is no way a man like Byron would even consider such a stunt (though since the 'niece' to whom he refers was Annabella Milbanke, whom Byron later did marry with disastrous results, things might have turned out better for both of them if he had).

Other members of the aristocracy, however, did not find the idea of advertising quite so ridiculous. In 1818, the second Lord Lucan, Richard Bingham, used *Galignani's* to announce that this 'descendant of the royal branches of Lorraine and Capet, and other sovereigns of Europe, wishes to contract an alliance with a lady capable from her rank and talents of supporting the dignity and titles, which an alliance so honourable would confer on her'. This was four years after he had formally separated from his controversial first wife, a divorcee named Elizabeth Belasyse. Presumably no suitable candidate presented herself, and in 1821 he had a daughter, Adele, by his

Italian lover Adelaide Gregorina. But Lucan did not give up hope of sharing his life with a woman more suitable to his rank: four years later, he tried again, placing a similar ad in the newspapers of Europe. This too failed to have the desired effect, and eventually, in 1837, he and Adelaide were married.

The real significance of Lord Lucan's antics was that they fuelled some women's hopes that the personal columns were populated by genuine aristocrats for whom it was more important that a wife

Richard Bingham, 2nd earl of Lucan, by Henry Bone, probably after Johan Joseph Zoffany (*c*.1812)

was pretty than rich, thus contributing to the myth that social mobility was possible — and even easy — for any woman who possessed the looks and the wit to manoeuvre herself into such a situation. It was an illusion, however, that, for a Suffolk mole-catcher's daughter named Maria Marten, was to have the most tragic of consequences.

Chapter Six

A Private Gentleman

THE FRONT PAGE of the 8 August 1828 edition of *The Times* contained the usual parade of classified ads: governesses and valets in search of employment, rooms for rent, horses for sale, ships about to set sail for the colonies, lost dogs. Turn to page two, however, and a very different story revealed itself. There was a lengthy account of the trial of William Corder, who brutally murdered his first wife and found his second wife through a Lonely Hearts ad. The trial generated a great deal of press interest, and the Red Barn murder (as it was commonly known) eventually became a cause célèbre, the subject of several books, plays and eventually a film. A local magistrate commented that he 'never knew or heard of a case in my life which abounded with so many extraordinary incidents as the present. It really appears more like a romance than a tale of common life; and were it not that the circumstances were so well authenticated, it would appear absolutely incredible; it, however, verifies the remark of Lord Byron that "Truth is stranger than fiction."' For the first time, Lonely Hearts ads were in the national spotlight.

William Corder was born in the village of Polstead in Suffolk in 1803, the son of a prosperous local farmer and his wife. At school, an early propensity for lying and stealing earned him the nickname Foxey. He later joined his five siblings working on the family's 300-acre farm. In appearance, he was fair-skinned with lots of freckles, very thin, and about five feet four inches tall, though he often seemed shorter because he walked with a stoop.

Corder's victim, Maria Marten, was born a couple of years before him, also in Polstead, the daughter of a mole-catcher named Thomas Marten and his wife Grace. Grace died when Maria was ten, so Maria took over the running of the household. She was generally considered a dedicated, honourable, bright and innocent girl, as well as a worryingly pretty one: 'Maria used to dress a little fine, and her sister, as well as [her stepmother] and her father, often quarrelled with her about it . . .' At the age of eighteen she began stepping out with a local boy named Thomas Corder — William's brother — and soon found herself pregnant. The baby only lived to be a few months old, and not long afterwards Thomas also died when he fell through the ice on a fishpond.

Maria then took up with another Polstead man, with whom she also had a baby; this one survived. But the relationship did not last, and it was then that she threw herself into her doomed liaison with

William Corder and Maria Marten. From *The Murder of Maria Marten* by J. Curtis (1828)

William Corder. '[A]n intimacy of a very close nature took place between them, and an illegitimate child was the fruit of it' was how *The Times* delicately described the circumstances that led to this unmarried girl of twenty-four giving birth for a third time (again, the baby died). Apparently the couple 'seemed always very fond of each other', though Maria's sister recalled that she did hear them argue over money a few times. Corder also used to taunt Maria about a rumour he claimed to have heard that the local constable was planning to arrest her for immoral behaviour (the constable was later to testify that this was not true).

Nonetheless, Corder repeatedly told Maria that he wanted to marry her; he was just a little vague as to when. Eventually they agreed that they would leave for Ipswich to get married on the evening of Wednesday, 16 May 1827. The trip was postponed twice: first due to Stoke fair, and then because Corder's brother James was taken ill. And so it was that at around noon on the Friday, Corder turned up at Maria's house. He made his way upstairs, where he found Maria in her bedroom with her stepmother, and insisted that

The Marten Cottage. From J. Curtis (1828)

she get ready to leave for Ipswich immediately in order to get married that very day.

'I am come – make haste – I am going,' said Corder.

'How can I go at this time of the day without any body seeing me?' Maria demanded.

'Never mind, we have been disappointed a good many times, and we will be disappointed no more.' Corder then repeated his claim that the local constable intended to arrest her.

'Oh William,' exclaimed Maria's stepmother Ann in exasperation, 'if you had but married Maria before this child was born, as I wished, all this would have been settled.'

'Well,' Corder replied, 'I am going to Ipswich to marry her tomorrow morning.'

'William, what will you do if that can't be done?' asked Ann.

'Don't make yourself uneasy, she shall be my lawful wife before I return, or I will get her a place till she can,' Corder reassured her. Maria continued to protest at the short notice – what bride does not want a little time to prepare for her wedding? – but eventually relented. And so Corder left her to pack.

When he returned a quarter of an hour later, he found that in order 'to escape observation', Maria had, as agreed, disguised herself as a man in a pair of blue trousers, a stripy waistcoat and a brown coat, with a green handkerchief tied around her neck; she also had a petticoat, stays, a chemise and jewellery on underneath. She left the house by a different door from Corder, with Ann acting as lookout, then the couple headed off in the direction of the Red Barn, an outbuilding on Corder's parents' farm. Ann testified that at this point Maria was 'crying and low-spirited'. It was the last time she was seen alive.

Early the following Sunday morning, Corder appeared at the Martens' cottage again, this time to inform her parents that the marriage had been delayed because they had to wait for the marriage licence to arrive from London. When Ann asked what Corder had done with Maria,

The Red Barn. From J. Curtis (1828)

he replied that she was lodged with a female relative of his in Yarmouth. But Ann remained suspicious, and with good reason. Maria's step-brother had spotted Corder at about four o'clock on that fateful Friday afternoon, walking through the fields from the Red Barn towards his mother's house carrying a pickaxe. Corder denied this, of course: 'It could not be me that he saw; it must have been Acres, who was employed that day in stubbing trees near the barn.' (Acres, a local farm-hand, later testified that this was a lie.) Corder remained in Polstead throughout the summer, claiming that Maria was still in Yarmouth, but that her family had received no letters from her first because she was too busy, and later because she had a sore on the back of her hand that meant she was unable to put pen to paper. He found it difficult to keep his story straight, however, at one point informing a neighbour that Maria had sailed to France aboard the steam-packet.

On 8 September, with harvest-time over – Corder personally supervised the stacking of all the corn into the Red Barn, no doubt to ensure that no untoward discoveries were made – he left Polstead, claiming that he had been diagnosed with consumption and advised to sojourn for a while somewhere warm by the sea. He headed for

Seaforth on the Isle of Wight and, following that, London. On 18 October, Maria's father received a postcard from him, in which Corder claimed that the wedding had now taken place.

Winter passed, and then spring, and still the Martens did not hear directly from Maria. On 19 April 1828, Thomas Marten searched the Red Barn – according to a later rumour, on account of a grisly vision that came to his wife in a dream. He poked around the barn's floor and before long 'came to the body, and near the head found the hand-kerchief tied round her neck apparently very tight. The body was lying

'William Corder as he appeared when in London'. From *An Accurate Account of the Trial of William Corder, for the Murder of Maria Marten* by George Foster (1828)

down, though not stretched out. The legs were drawn up, and the head bent down into the earth.' There was no doubt that it was Maria. She had been shot in the head, stabbed in the heart and strangled with her own handkerchief.

Suspicion immediately fell upon William Corder, who had been merrily building a new life for himself. After some months lodging at the Bull Inn on Leadenhall Street, he began to crave some domestic comfort and decided to look for a wife. This was not an easy task. He was new to the city and had no friends and few acquaintances there. And so, on 13 November 1827, he announced his intention to readers of the *Morning Herald*:

> Matrimony. A Private Gentleman, aged 24, entirely independent, whose disposition is not to be exceeded, has lately lost the chief of his family by the hand of Providence, which has occasioned discord among the remainder, under circumstances most disagreeable to relate. To any female of respectability, who would study for domestic comfort, and willing to confide her future happiness in one every way qualified to render the marriage state desirable, as the advertiser is in affluence. The lady must have the power of some property, which may remain in her own possession. Many very happy marriages have taken place through means similar to this now resorted to, and it is hoped that no one will answer this through impertinent curiosity; but should this meet the eye of any agreeable lady, who feels desirous of meeting with a sociable, tender, kind and sympathising companion, they will find this advertisement worthy of notice. Honour and secrecy may be relied on. As some little security against idle applications, it is requested that letters may be addressed (post-paid) to A.Z. care of Mr Foster, stationer, No. 68, Leadenhall Street, which will meet with the most respectful attention.

With the oblique reference to 'circumstances most disagreeable to relate', Corder cunningly discouraged people from investigating his family situation too closely. Instead, he emphasised qualities like his 'disposition' and his 'affluence', thus presenting himself in an appealing light at the same time as demanding very little of a prospective wife, save that she had some property and was respectable.

Corder asked for all replies to be sent to George Foster's stationery shop, which was just down the road from the Bull Inn. Foster was soon deluged with letters: there were forty-five in response to the ad in the *Herald*, plus another fifty-three in response to another ad in the *Sunday Times* a couple of weeks later. Thus Corder could reasonably have boasted of almost a hundred women all keen to become Mrs Corder without even having met him.

None of the fifty-three letters that arrived in reply to the *Sunday Times* ad were collected, however. For months they sat underneath the shop counter, gathering dust. It was not until after Corder's trial that they finally saw the light of day, when Foster published them in what was to become a best-selling book. Taken together, they demonstrate how difficult it is to generalise about the sort of women who replied to Lonely Hearts ads. From the poor and illiterate to the wealthy and well-educated, the only thing that unites them is the courage (although some might call it recklessness) they demonstrate in approaching this unknown suitor in the first place.

Thirteen of the women are so concerned that the ad might not be genuine that they offer Corder no personal details whatsoever. Those who do are all aged between eighteen and twenty-six; the majority are either twenty-two or twenty-three. Two are the daughters of tradesmen in the midst of financial difficulties. Another is one of a clergyman's eight children. One has just acquired a stepmother: 'there is a second family, therefore to prevent any disagreement amongst us, I have left my father's house'. There is a teacher, a high-class shop assistant and a lady's companion who has recently experienced 'misfortunes of a painful and pecuniary nature'. Three

are widows, three are orphans and another three live solely with their
mothers following the death of their father: 'my prospects like many
others in this life have been greatly blighted, through loss of a parent
. . .' One letter arrived from Kent; the rest came from London.

One of the letters is littered with bad spelling and grammar, but
the rest appear to have been written by entirely respectable, even
genteel women. Since Corder's ad specifically mentioned 'domestic
comfort', many boast of their prowess on the domestic front. Other
adjectives that crop up again and again include 'amiable', 'affectionate',
'cheerful', 'educated' and 'respectable'. 'Amiable' in particular appears
in almost every letter. Two also mention how musical they are (piano
and voice). Very few describe their physical appearance, but those
who do range from the overly honest ('of rather short stature, slight
made, not handsome, dark complexion, dark hair and eyes') to the
somewhat conceited ('In person I am considered a pretty little figure.
Hair nut-brown, blue eyes, not generally considered plain').

The group contains one nineteen-year-old who replied to Corder's
ad out of a romantic sense that she wants to hold out for her Mr
Right. She describes how '. . . my father has received an offer from
one whose disposition is in every respect the opposite of my own,
I cannot accept it only by sacrificing every feeling of delicacy and
affection'. Approaching Corder was 'the only means that presented'
itself of 'preventing the sacrifice of my own happiness'. She was
not alone in expressing her agreement with Corder that many a
successful marriage had been arranged through a newspaper.

The majority, however, replied to the ad out of a profound desperation to escape an unhappy home life. As well as a preponderance of
orphans and widows, there are those who will have no money of their
own until one or both parents die. There are also a few in a predicament similar to the teacher in 'a respectable school' who was keenly
aware that 'without property or a home, I have not the opportunity
of obtaining a suitable companion'. Others are a little more poetic
when explaining their current circumstances: 'My prospects in life

were once brilliant, but when misfortune with her gloomy train of attendants surrounded my family, the scene changed ...' This was the plight of 'no giddy girl, nor am I a romantic old maid, but a warm hearted affectionate girl' of twenty-one. Clearly the options for young, single women without independent means remained severely limited.

Of all the letters that the postman delivered to George Foster's stationery shop, none is sadder than the one from a twenty-two-year-old with 'not the least pretension to beauty, quite the contrary'. Her parents had died when she was very young and she had been sent away to school to train as a governess. Some years later, she found herself pregnant but unwed, the result, she explained, of 'deviation from rectitude, which was occasioned by the too easily listening to the flattery of one, whose vows I foolishly believed to be true ...' She had fallen victim to 'an affection which I supposed to be mutual, and at the same time honourable, but alas have found it to be quite the reverse'. The result was 'a sweet little girl, who is my greatest comfort, she is sixteen months old, and is beginning to prattle very prettily'. In order to support herself and her daughter, she had begun to take in needlework, but it was proving a struggle, not least because 'I am entirely deserted by my family, and banished from society'. 'I do not altogether merit such a fate,' she protests, 'for I do assure you, that no one could have acted more prudently than I have done since the unfortunate circumstance happened, which has very much destroyed my peace of mind, but I still hope to see better days ...' This sense of 'hope' is, after all, what Lonely Hearts ads are all about.

It is not surprising to discover that many of these women had misgivings about finding a husband via this highly unconventional method: 'Feelingly alive to the general received opinion of the impropriety of answering ads, I will for once swerve and reply to yours.' Some claim to have seen the ad 'by accident' or 'inadvertedly' or to have had it 'pointed out' to them. They admit to a sense of 'repugnance' at replying to it, emphasising that they have not told family or friends: 'this letter is unknown to any one, and should we eventually become acquainted, I should not wish it known even to my own family the way in which the acquaintance was formed'. Others profess a concern that the author of the ad might turn out to be a fortune-hunter or a con-artist. Little did they suspect that the truth was far, far worse.

Many, however, threw caution to the wind. They were so anxious to make Corder's acquaintance that they sought to arrange a tryst immediately. One asked him to meet her on the south side of Northampton Square between 12 p.m. and 1 p.m. the following Monday; he was to hold a white handkerchief in his hand to iden-tify himself. Another, an orphan, evidences the lack of parental guidance in her life by inviting him to visit her at home the very next afternoon. Others resort to subterfuge:

> Sir,
>
> ... I am of a respectable family, my papa having seen a reverse of fortune, has occasioned my mamma to enter into a boarding house at —— which, if it meets your approbation, will thank you to call to-morrow evening between four and five o'clock, as it will be the most likely time of seeing me. This being unknown to my parents, you had better come as if for boarding. I have a sister at home with me, who is twenty-one, my age is twenty-two. I must beg to excuse this bad writing, as it is done in fear.

Taken together, what these letters reveal is the immensely high level of demand for husbands: the country swarmed with socially and sexually unfulfilled and frustrated middle-class women, truly desperate for a way out.

And these are just the letters that Corder never got around to collecting. Those he did collect included one from a Miss Moore, who lived just off London's Gray's Inn Road with her mother and brother, who was a jeweller. In what one journalist suspected was 'a quixotic and preconcerted plan between the parties', Corder first met Miss Moore on the Isle of Wight in the autumn, and he then bumped into her again in a Fleet Street pastry shop a few weeks later. It was only when she replied to his ad, though, that romance flourished. A week later the couple were married at St Andrew's church in Holborn, and they then set up home at Grove House on Ealing Lane in Brentford, where they established a school for young ladies, ironically enough. Mrs Corder had no idea of her husband's past, and was said to worship him.

Unfortunately for Corder, it was at around this time that the body of Maria Marten was discovered. At ten o'clock on the morning of 22 April 1828, Constable James Lea knocked vigorously on the front door of Grove House. Corder opened it in his dressing-gown (he had been timing some boiled eggs for breakfast) and ushered the constable into the drawing-room. Lea asked him three times if

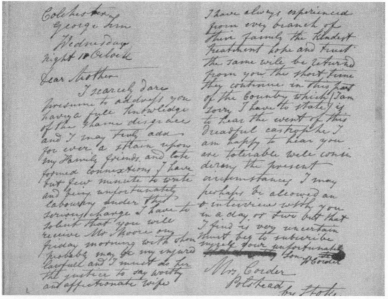

A letter William Corder wrote to his mother on his way to Bury gaol. From *The Trial of William Corder* by Knight & Lacey (1828)

William Corder in his cell in Bury
gaol. From J. Curtis (1828)

he knew Maria Marten, and three times Corder denied any knowledge of her. He was then arrested.

The trial of William Corder for the murder of Maria Marten
opened in Bury St Edmunds on 7 August 1828. So many people
turned up at the courthouse to watch that, when the doors were
flung open, the crowd poured in 'with a force so tremendous as to
risk the limbs of those who were not sufficiently athletic for active
personal resistance'. The judge, Lord Chief Baron Alexander, was
literally swept off his feet as he attempted to make his way to his
seat. In the opinion of the journalist covering the story for *The
Times*, it was 'a scene of confusion and uproar exceeding any thing
hitherto observed in trials of this nature'.

Corder pleaded not guilty. He admitted that he had arranged to
meet Maria Marten in the Red Barn, but claimed they had an argument and she shot herself in a passion. But even he was unable to
provide a satisfactory explanation of the strangulation and the stab

wounds, feebly proposing that perhaps she got them from the spade that was used to search for her body. Throughout the trial, emotions ran high. When Maria's stepmother was called to the witness box to identify some items of clothing, she 'was so overpowered, either by her feelings, by the effluvia of the rags, or by the heat of the court, that she was with difficulty preserved from fainting by the restoratives given her at the close of her examination'.

When it came to summing up the case, the judge drew attention to various inconsistencies in the prisoner's story, in particular the claim that Maria had committed suicide. 'It often happened that these poor girls, when disappointed in their expectation, did lay rash hands on themselves [but it] was extraordinary that instead of hanging herself upon a tree, as poor girls usually did in such circumstances, she should have used two different means to kill herself.' The jury 'must decide how far it was possible that such multifarious wounds were inflicted by herself'. This they did, and it took them just thirty-five minutes to reach a verdict: Guilty. The judge immediately sentenced Corder to be hanged.

The next day, as Corder sat in his prison cell awaiting execution, he received a visit from his wife. According to *The Times*, he asked just one thing of her: that if she decided to marry again, it should not be someone she met through a Lonely Hearts ad, 'for it was of all modes of getting a husband the most dangerous and imprudent'. It is likely, however, that this is more moralising on the part of the newspaper than a solid piece of reporting.

Although 11 August was a Monday, many in Bury St Edmunds had taken the day off work in order to attend the greatest spectacle in town: Corder's execution. By 9 a.m. 1,000 people had showed up; by midday the numbers had swelled to more than 7,000. At 11.50 a.m., Corder was escorted out of his prison cell. 'May God forgive me! Lord receive my soul!' he was heard to mumble repeatedly as he ascended the scaffold, from where the view was rather beautiful, had he had a mind to notice it: in the distance were rolling hills, and beyond them farmlands. 'I deserve my fate! I have offended my God. May he have mercy on my soul!' the condemned man muttered as the hangman placed the cap over his face. And with that, the ground disappeared from beneath his feet, and he swung free.

Corder's body was then cut down and transported by cart to the Shire Hall, where it was laid out for the public to inspect, which (according to the local paper) more than 5,000 people did on the first day alone. Outside, hawkers sold off the rope used to hang him for a guinea an inch. His skeleton was put on display at the museum at the Royal College of Surgeons (where it remained until 2004), while his skin was used to bind a book that can still be seen at Moyse's Hall Museum in Bury St Edmunds.

William Corder's trial and execution for the Red Barn murder were covered in feverish detail by both the national and local press. Thomas Hardy even read about it in his local newspaper as far away as Dorset. *The Times* in particular went to town: murder, matrimonial ads, bastard children – what more could a scandal-hungry newspaperman ask for? Its coverage was astonishingly intrusive, including, for example, the publication of a private copy of a letter Corder wrote to his wife the morning of his execution. *The Times's* reporter J. Curtis was also the author of one of a number of books on the case, and his belief that it had 'more the appearance of a melo-dramatic romance than an occurrence in a civilized country like England' was one with which many concurred: plays about the murder were among the most frequently performed melodramas of the century.

But this was not merely some 'melo-dramatic romance'. This was real life. For years, many of the anxieties that society harboured about Lonely Hearts ads had been played out on Drury Lane in the form of farce. But they were no longer a laughing matter. In 1828, they were personified in William Corder. The result was that the existence of Lonely Hearts ads became firmly embedded in the public consciousness. The month the murder took place, May, also saw the repeal of the Test and Corporation Acts. With Roman

Catholics no longer barred from public office, a central element of the old order had been symbolically shattered. This anticipated other major changes to come: the following year saw the repeal of all other Protestant privileges, while the Reform Act of 1832 dramatically shifted the political landscape towards a more democratic bent. Teetering on the cusp between the Georgian and the Victorian eras, Britain thus found itself in the midst of a national identity crisis.

This was reflected in the press coverage of the Red Barn murder, infused as it was with the sort of moral confusion that typified this 'age of cant', as some historians have characterised it. *The Times* used a leader piece to 'congratulate the country on a manifest improvement in the condition of its moral feeling'. It cast Corder as a figure of pure evil: he 'has united in this one deed of horror – if it be his only one – whatever the heart revolts at most in the conduct of man to woman. He seduced – then betrayed – then massacred the wretched creature, in cold blood ...' Corder was depicted as a predatory gentleman farmer preying on a virginal country girl, while Maria's moral slips (three children by three different men, none of whom she was married to) went all but ignored. It made for a better story, after all. The fact that Corder had then gone on to place a Lonely Hearts ad only provided further ammunition:

> There may be here and there a platonic lover, a quixotic senti-
> mentalist or a *timid being*, who might resort to such a measure;
> but ... Our experience is, and it is founded upon consider-
> able experience, arising from a long acquaintance with the
> public press, that those advertisements generally emanate from
> speculative, sensual and sordid men, whose aim is to obtain a
> *mistress*, or a *fortune*, rather than a wife.

'Detestable,' the reporter for *The Times* called it. 'Unmanly.'

The print media reserved its most intense censure, however, for the women who replied to Corder's ad. According to *The Times*, Corder, 'by twice puffing his personal qualities in a lying ad, turned the heads of 98 indiscreet spinsters, silly boarding-school girls, or wanton widows'. This was not at all an accurate description of the women involved, but it was based on an assumption that had by now become so engrained in the public consciousness that few chose to veer from it. George Foster in his account of 1828 accused the women of lacking 'maiden modesty', while the journalist J. Curtis asserted that for them '. . . to notice the trash of a Matrimonial Advertisement is to depart from the delicacy of their sex . . .' Maria Marten was asking for it, was the gist of it. *The Times* queried, 'Why will not unhappy females bethink themselves before it be too late, that he who is depraved enough to corrupt their innocence, has already made no small advances in that course which ends too often in his exacting from them the only remaining sacrifice?' In other words, any man depraved enough to use a Lonely Hearts ad to meet women was also the kind of man who probably wanted to murder them as well.

But what choice did these women have? The 'Situations Wanted' ads in *The Times* on 8 August 1828, the second day of Corder's trial, featured, among others, 'A Lady of the greatest respectability who has been for many years accustomed to tuition [who] wishes to obtain a situation in a Nobleman's or highly respectable Family' and 'A Widow, under 30 years of age, from cheerful disposition, but very small income, [who] would be happy to meet with a Lady of similar description to join her in taking a small cottage at or near some watering-place . . .' There is also what is in all likelihood a veiled Lonely Hearts ad: 'A young widow lady wishes for a situation to superintend the domestic affairs of a single Gentleman or Widower'. Taken together, these ads vividly demonstrate the tragically limited options that were available to respectable women without independent means. A paradox is laid bare: in attempting to exert some element of control over their future – by putting themselves on the open market – these women were simultaneously making themselves vulnerable to all manner of patriarchal exploitation, or worse.

TO PARENTS and GUARDIANS.—WANTED, a respectable well-educated Youth, as an APPRENTICE to a Printer and Stationer, in a Dissenter's family. The house is an old established one, free of the Stationers' Company, and will be found very eligible for a well disposed youth of about 14. Further particulars by applying to X. Y., at Mr. Stone's, 9, Skinner-street, Snow-hill: if by letter, post paid.

TO SCHOOL ASSISTANTS.—An ASSISTANT, accustomed to teach writing and arithmetic, is immediately WANTED, in a small School, in the immediate vicinity of town. Unexceptionable testimonials of character and ability will be required. Cards of address may be obtained of Mr. Denney, 38, Barbican.

GOVERNESS.—In the Family of a Clergyman is WANTED a Lady, to TEACH a Child, 7 years of age, to read, speak, and write the French language correctly. A native of France would be preferred, who will be treated as one of the family. A moderate salary would be given at first, which must be stated in letters, post paid, to A. B. Z., postoffice, Bicester, Oxfordshire.

A YOUNG LADY, of respectable connexions, in her 18th year, who has been accustomed to teach the junior pupils English, French, &c., wishes for a SITUATION as UNDER TEACHER. Her friends would have no objection to give a small premium for the first year, or pay the masters for their instructions. Address to M.A., 13, Thornton-street, Dock-head.

A YOUNG LADY, who has resided on the Conti- nent, and has been for some years accustomed to tuition, is desirous of meeting with a SITUATION in a private family, to undertake the education of two or three young Ladies. She is competent to instruct in the English and French languages, writing, arithmetic, dancing, the rudiments of music, and the use of the globes. The most respectable references can be given. Address, post paid, to A.Z., 51, Totton-street, Stepney.

GOVERNESS.—A young Lady, of the Established Church, is desirous of obtaining a SITUATION as GOVERNESS in a Family, where the age of the pupils does not exceed 13 years, or as Teacher in a respectable School. She is competent to instruct in the English, French, and Italian languages, geography, music, history, writing, arithmetic, algebra, geometry, &c., with the use of the globes, &c. The most satisfactory reference can be given. Address, post paid, to V. X., Mr. Armstrong's, 36, King-street, West Smithfield.

A LADY, residing in a genteel and healthy situa- tion, near town, who receives a limited number of young Ladies, undertakes to INSTRUCT in every branch of useful and ornamental education, together with music, French, and drawing. Terms for board and instruction, including accomplishments, 30 guineas per annum. No extra charges will be made for books, washing, drawing materials, or stationery, it being the intention of the advertiser not to exceed the stipulated sum. A small select library is provided for the use of the pupils. The most unexceptionable references can be given. Address, post paid, to Mr. Ariel, 51, Holborn-hill.

A LADY of the greatest respectability, who has been for many years accustomed to tuition, wishes to obtain a SITUATION in a Nobleman's or highly respectable Family, or as Principal Assistant in a first-rate Seminary. The advertiser is fully competent to instruct her pupils in all the useful and polite branches of an accomplished education without the assistance of masters, including English, French, geography with the use of the globes, writing, arithmetic, drawing, painting on velvet, wood, glass, &c., together with all descriptions of useful and ornamental works. The most satisfactory references will be given. Address, post paid, to P. H., 16, Princes-street, Soho.

AT a genteel ESTABLISHMENT, in a pleasant watering-place, in the west of England, where the society is cheerful and highly respectable, there are Vacancies for two or three young Ladies as PARLOUR BOARDERS. Terms and references may be had on application at 23, Threadneedle-street; or by letter, post paid, directed to X. Z., postoffice, Blandford.

PRIVATE EDUCATION.—A married Lady, without family, of English parents, and of the Established Church, but born and educated in Paris, having been accustomed to tuition for the last 14 years, is desirous of devoting her time to the education of 3 or 4 young Ladies. The strictest care will be paid to their health, principles, instruction, and manners. French constantly spoken. Most respectable references will be given. Cards of address at Mr. Fricker's circulating library, 3, Little Ormond-street, Queen-square.

SELECT BOARDING SCHOOL.—A Clergyman of Oxford, well qualified, who conducts an establishment of this description for a limited number of pupils, in an admired environ of London, has one VACANCY. Parents who wish for a seminary where the pupils receive the principal's daily personal instruction, partake of meals at the same table with his family, and have their morals, manners, and religious duties conscientiously attended to, will find this an eligible school for their sons. Terms moderate. Satisfactory references will be given. Address, post paid, with signature D. D., at Mr. Bowen's, stationer, 315, Oxford-street.

TO PARENTS.——A Widow Lady and her Daughter, who has been teacher in a school some years, residing in a most delightful and healthy situation, 6 miles from town, wish to take four CHILDREN, in addition to two they have at present, to BOARD and INSTRUCT in the usual branches of education. The greatest care will be taken, and the most kind treatment experienced. Stages to town every hour. The most respectable references given. Terms moderate. Address, post paid, to R. G., at Mr. Hill's, 115, Wood-street, Cheapside; or to Mr. Menniss, Talbot-court, Gracechurch-street.

A YOUNG MAN, from the country, aged 20, who writes an excellent hand, wishes a SITUATION as CLERK, Warehouseman, Shopman, or in any capacity where he can make himself useful. Can give undeniable references. Apply at 26, Threadneedle-street.

TO WATCHMAKERS and JEWELLERS.— WANTED, by a young Man of respectability, a SITUATION in a Retail Watchmaker's Jeweller's, and Engraver's Shop. Can make himself generally useful in all its branches. Satisfactory reference will be given. Apply to Mr. Davis, 8, Worship-street, Finsbury-square.

PARTNERSHIP.—To a Gentleman and man of business, commanding £5,000, a highly advantageous opportunity presents itself of embarking his capital in a concern which realizes from 35 to 40 per cent. Letters, with real name and address, from principals only, directed, post free, to W. L., at the Hambro' coffeehouse, Water-lane, Tower-street.

APPRENTICESHIP.—To Wholesale Tradesmen and Others.—The Friends of a Youth, who has been well-educated, wish to APPRENTICE him to a respectable Business, where he would be treated liberally, and attention paid to his improvement. A premium will be given. A Freeman of the City would be preferred. Address, post paid, to R. J., at Mr. Jones's, cutler, 9, Finsbury-place.

AS GROOM or VALET to a single Gentleman, or Groom in a small private family, a young Man, aged 24, who can command a six years' character from the situation which he is on the point of leaving. Address to George Kinsey, at Messrs. Powell and Son's, veterinary surgeons, Webb-street, Bermondsey-street. All letters to be post paid.

TO MERCHANTS, &c.—A young Man, who writes a fine expeditious hand, is well acquainted with bookkeeping and the general routine of business, is desirous of meeting with a SITUATION in a Merchant's or Tradesman's COUNTINGHOUSE. Most respectable references can be given. Address, post paid, to A. B., 44, Little Eastcheap.

LAW.—WANTS a SITUATION, in a Solicitor's Office, a Gentleman of respectable connexions, who has for a number of years exclusively managed the Conveyancing and Chancery departments in an office of considerable practice, and who would undertake the management of either or both of those departments. Address to A.B., Mr. Lodar's, 5, Southampton-buildings, Chancery-lane.

TO LINENDRAPERS.—WANTED, a SITUA- TION, for a Youth, 15 years of age, who has been some time in a linendraper's shop, and is capable of making himself very useful to his employer. He is respectably connected, of good morals, has been religiously educated, is very steady, and writes a good hand. A small salary would satisfy. Apply to J. B., at 370, Oxford-street.

SERVANT of ALL-WORK.—WANTED, a strong active YOUNG WOMAN, well acquainted with every branch of household work, who can cook, wash, iron, milk, make butter, and do every thing required, in a small family where a cow is kept. None need apply who cannot have a most unexceptionable character. Liberal wages will be given. Apply at Mr. Brackett's library, Powis-street, Woolwich.

PARTNERSHIP.—A Gentleman of respectable connexions, who has been accustomed to mercantile pursuits, and has the command of from £2,000 to £3,000, is desirous of joining as PARTNER a respectable and well-established Concern, to which he would give his whole time and attention. The most unexceptionable references will be given and required. Letters, post paid, with particulars, to be addressed to L. S., Mr. Wright's, 10, Southampton-street, Camden-town.

LAW PARTNERSHIP.—A Gentleman, who has served his clerkship, and has since passed some years as pupil with an eminent conveyancer, is desirous of meeting with a PARTNERSHIP in a house of established practice, to which he conceives he could offer considerable advantages. The references which he can give are of the very highest class, both as to abilities and legal information. His connexions are highly respectable, and would be able to increase the business of the office. Apply (if by letter, post paid, to W. A. H.) at Mr. Wilkinson's, law stationer, 49, Coleman-street.

TO WHOLESALE HOUSES in the DRUG BUSINESS.—An ENGAGEMENT WANTED, as TRAVELLER, by a Gentleman well acquainted with the drug business, who is desirous to represent a house of the first respectability. This opportunity offers great advantages to a house desirous of extending their connexion generally, and particularly amongst medical men. Remuneration not the principal object. The highest references can be given, as well as ample security. The advertiser is prepared, at a short notice, to proceed upon a journey. Address, post paid, to X.Y.Z., postoffice, Brighton.

MORTGAGE.—WANTED, the SUM of £800, on MORTGAGE of 17 newly-erected Leasehold Houses, producing a net rental of £120; 70 years of the lease are unexpired. The borrower would either pay off the principal by six yearly instalments, or take the money for 6 years certain. Address to R. F., at Messrs. Culsha and Mason's, Threadneedle-street.

HOUSE WANTED, Furnished or Unfurnished. —WANTED, a small genteel HOUSE, Furnished or Unfurnished, within four miles of the Royal Exchange; it must have 2 sitting rooms, and not less than 4 bed rooms. Applications, with full particulars, to be addressed, post paid, to C. B. A., at Batson's coffeehouse, Cornhill.

From the front page of *The Times*, 8 August 1828

Chapter Seven

Puffs for Adventurers

And why, pray, should not a woman look into a newspaper to find a husband as well as to learn the fashion of a bonnet? ... there is something very delightful and romantic about these newspaper matches. First, there is the charming uncertainty ... What kind of person has he? What colour his eyes? ... Delightful speculations! Oh, there is something really admirable in such ads! I could feast upon them all day!

SO BEGINS THE play *Wives by Advertisement: or, Courting in the news-papers* by the popular dramatist Douglas Jerrold, which premiered at the Royal Coburg Theatre (now the Old Vic) in September 1828, just a month after William Corder's execution. The play's subject matter cannily capitalised on what had suddenly become a major topic of discussion at dinner tables all over the country: exactly why were Lonely Hearts ads such an enduring feature of modern British society? What many found particularly amazing was the sheer number of apparently respectable women who had replied to the murderer's ad. In the wake of the intensive newspaper coverage of the case, people wanted answers.

Jerrold was right that, for some, Lonely Hearts ads were simply a bit of fun. Far more people read them than actually responded to them, after all. British society in the first half of the nineteenth century decreed that respectable women like Laura, the play's heroine who speaks the above words, spend an inordinate amount of time confined to the home, so a few minutes spent reading the ads in the newspaper was as good a way as any to pass a morning. In describing them as 'Delightful speculations!' Laura relates them to the sort of economic speculation in the stock market that, in the late 1820s, was becoming increasingly widespread. Whether speculating for money or for men, both brought a thrill.

The Corder case, however, exposed the fact that some women did more than just read the ads: they responded to them, even in the years immediately after the case. For the marriage market continued to be regulated via an increasingly elaborate code of social etiquette, and this presented a number of hurdles to genteel women in search of a husband. Few public places were open to a woman who was on her own, especially if she was under thirty. Without a chaperone there was no possibility of attending the theatre, a dance or dinner in a restaurant. Furthermore, from the 1830s onwards an ever-intensifying focus on domestic values meant that the social life of the middle and upper classes centred more and more around the home. When young women paid social calls, they had to be accompanied by their parents and were not permitted to spend any time alone with a suitor; men were allowed to pay a return visit, but only once the relationship was deemed serious, and even then just on Sundays. The crux of the problem was, in short, the 'present rule of drawing-room duplicity'.

This magnificent phrase is drawn from a pamphlet published in 1832 entitled *Some remarks on matrimonial advertisements*. Its author, known only as Y.M., criticised 'the forced and exclusive state of our society', going on to rail against 'the social, or rather unsocial state of England, where females are shut out from all opportunity of advancing their own interest'. Those who disapprove of Lonely Hearts ads have 'been schooled in prudery', and, indeed, prudery was one of the defining characteristics of Britain under William IV. Y.M. harboured an ulterior motive in his defence of Lonely Hearts ads, however. The pamphlet was also an extended puff for his own

Love in a Maze by John Leech: an attempt to elude the dreaded, ever-present chaperone

recently established marriage agency, which over the course of the next five years regularly placed ads in the London papers on behalf of the many men and women whom Y.M. claimed to have on his books.

Y.M. does offer up a possible solution to the stigma that surrounded Lonely Hearts ads: '. . . by a thousand harmless strata-gems the intimacy can be made to wear the appearance of having begun in accident, or an arranged party enables the lady to account for it to her friends'. He gives the example of one client whose new husband 'has been so far deceived, that he supposed her family private acquaintances of my own, and that they had no knowledge of the paragraph which attracted his notice. I have seen him marry, I know him to be happy, I am sure he is grateful; and, up to the present hour, he dreams not how the whole originated . . .' The conclusion? 'If two persons are known to be of established reputation and private worth, can the *mere mode* of introduction make them otherwise?' He has a point.

Although women continued to reply to ads enthusiastically, between about 1800 and 1870 very few actually placed ads themselves. This was just one consequence of renewed limitations on female self-determination in this period. There was an expanded concern for manners and morals, with the emergence in the 1830s of a new genre of literature known as etiquette books (as opposed to conduct books, which had been around for centuries). In general, women were expected to exist only within the private sphere – that is, at home. Those who actively courted a public existence were deemed by some to be no better than a common prostitute. Thus to place an ad in a newspaper, even an anonymous one, and thereby not only declare one's desires openly, but also thrust oneself forward into the public sphere, was to thumb one's nose at social convention. It required a willingness to defy the rules that, understandably, few women found themselves able to conjure up.

As a result, three decades into the century almost the only Lonely Hearts ads from women that appeared in the press were fake ones. 'A matrimonial advertisement is a sort of steam vehicle on the railroad to matrimony' was the verdict of *Fraser's Magazine*, which in April 1835 dedicated an entire issue to the letters it received in response to an ad it placed in a London newspaper in the name of research that purported to be from a 'young lady, just of age, born in India, of highly respectable family and connexions, [who] determines rather to take a highly unfeminine step than to be hurried into a match repugnant to her sensibility'.

The most interesting revelation, in the magazine's view, was that almost all the replies were from 'men of rank and family'. First up was a soldier, 'a gentleman of the very first connexions', who professed a penchant for 'a tolerable foot and ancle [*sic*], and good long eye-lashes'. Next was 'Werter' from Brighton – thirty years old, six foot tall, dark hair – who proclaimed that 'it is necessary to my very existence that I should see you, converse with you, know you ... My heart actually glows with affection!' There was a twenty-eight-year-old civil servant who preferred sitting by the fireside reading poetry to 'whirling into the vortex of midnight pleasure', a clergy-man, a German philosophy scholar, a lieutenant in the navy on £100 a year who 'shall be happy to take you in tow into the port of Matrimony' and an Irishman with four brothers who wrote from the Jerusalem Coffee-House since he was about to leave London for the Swan River in western Australia and would like a wife to take with him. There was also a Byron-obsessed graduate of Trinity College, Cambridge, who was currently a private in the Life Guards who pleaded, 'Exhort this horrid scribble – it is our best orderly-room pens and paper!'

Men also placed ads with gusto, despite the fact that in doing so they were effectively aligning themselves with the murderer Corder. Late 1828 and early 1829 actually saw a spike in ads: all publicity really is good publicity, it seems. The coverage of the trial appears to have had the unexpected effect not of deterring men from adver-tising for a wife, but rather of serving to remind or even inform them that this existed as a viable option. It had led Corder to the loyal and respectable Miss Moore, after all.

The strictures of nineteenth-century society made it more awkward and embarrassing than ever for men to make the first move, as they were universally expected to. As a result, according to an advertiser in 1831, 'The Press is become now, for the most delicate of all businesses, a securer channel of transaction than the drawing-room; for it carries the most sincere appeal to the inmost recesses of congenial hearts, uninterrupted and unsuspected . . .' The following year, the aforementioned Y.M. expressed his sympathy for those who found it difficult to approach the female sex: 'It never occurs to [ladies], that a man may be deterred by an imaginary something from encountering the caprices of coquetry, or the pains and penalties of a mortifying repulse . . . They seem not aware, that thousands of noble spirit in the field, are constitutionally timid in female society . . .'

Y.M. reserves special pity for two particular groups of men: first, the 'hundreds of young and beneficed clergymen, confined to remote villages and a limited circle, [who] have no one of corresponding rank and education near them', and then

> the officers and civilians in the service of His Majesty, and the Hon. East India Company, who have been absent in distant and unsocial climes from the first dawn of manhood. Returning, if indeed they chance to survive the customary period, they find themselves without the female associates of their youth, or the means, for want of introduction of acquiring others in their stead.

As Britain expanded its empire abroad, more and more men found themselves facing this very problem, as evidenced in ads of the period, such as the one from 'An officer of distinguished rank and service, in the Bengal army, about to leave England for Calcutta and Upper India, whither he purposes travelling for pleasure for a couple of years, prior to his retirement from the service', who sought 'a lady of education and good family' to accompany him.

Y.M. also highlights an increasingly common obstacle to courtship: 'thousands, occupied in their different professions, really have no time to devote to it'. This is borne out by many an actual ad, for example the tradesman in 1841 'who being much occupied in business, and not knowing in the rather limited circle of his acquaintance a lady suited to his taste and circumstances, takes this (though to some minds questionable, but as he thinks) legitimate method of supplying the deficiency of his circumscribed connection'.

To add to the challenges faced by a single man in search of a wife, as the Industrial Revolution gained pace, the urban population of Britain grew and grew. The census of 1851 revealed that, for the first time, more people lived in cities than in the countryside; London alone had an estimated 2.4 million people. As one young buck explained in his ad, 'London, though so large, is, as to sociability, a desert to a great many; and it often renders single life exceedingly heavy, and marriages difficult, for the frequent mutual unfitness of limited chance acquaintances.' No doubt many today would agree with this assessment of life in the capital, which is – and always has been – an existence of chance encounters, random connections and superficial interactions. It is a state of affairs brought vividly to life by the central protagonist, Robert Audley, in Mary Braddon's 1862 novel, *Lady Audley's Secret*:

That girl on the kerbstone yonder, waiting to cross the street when my chariot shall have passed, may be the one woman out of every female creature in this vast universe who could make me a happy man. Yet I pass her by – bespatter her with the mud from my wheels, in my helpless ignorance, in my blind submission to the awful hand of fatality.

Life in the world's first urbanised society could be intensely lonely. When at work, most people were too busy toiling away to remember to wink at the proprietor's pretty daughter; while church, which had once been a popular place for the sexes to mingle, was no longer so well attended, now that many people's parents lived too far away to bully them into going. It was a world made up of strangers, and the

A busy London street (1862)

sense of isolation could overwhelm one within hours of passing
through the Islington turnpike from the north. On the plus side, it
meant that there were fewer nosy neighbours or interfering relatives
around to scrutinise one's behaviour. Many were thus liberated to
hunt high and low for love, in whatever way and in whatever place
they chose, with little or no fear of the social consequences that
might have plagued them back home in a watchful rural community.

A letter to the *Bristol Mercury* in 1837 detailed a cavalcade of unfortunate experiences arising from a Lonely Hearts ad, many of them
the result of the logistical difficulties of city life. The recent increases
in the volume of overseas trade meant that Bristol was booming,
and migrants were flooding there in search of jobs; the population
increased fivefold over the course of the century. Yet this did not
help this particular bachelor gentleman to get himself hitched, and
at the age of forty he decided to advertise. Following up on one
of the replies, he found himself dressed in his best frock-coat waiting
under a lamp post at six o'clock one Tuesday evening, holding a

black walking-stick in one hand and a glove in the other, just as he had been instructed to. His date soon arrived and, while at first conversation was a bit strained, things quickly improved. He was much impressed when she revealed that she lived with a Lady Courtly.

'As her friend?'

'Not exactly' she replied, and changed the subject. Six dates later he decided to marry her, but, on opening preliminary negotiations, it transpired that she was merely Lady Courtly's servant, and as a result he broke off the relationship immediately.

This was the trouble with Lonely Hearts ads: by meeting someone entirely out of context, protected by the anonymity of city life and separated from the connections of their kin, with all the potential for reinvention that this entailed, there was no way of knowing that anyone really was who they said they were. Our Bristol bachelor's luck did not improve: having placed a second ad, he received one lovely reply, but when he met up with the lady in person he 'found her features of a kind to which no length of time can reconcile the beholder'. With another, he travelled all the way to York to meet her, waited at the appointed place every night for three weeks and still she never turned up. And this was not even the worst of it. 'At another time, I was directed to cross a certain meadow, but, just as I was entering it, found myself up to the neck in mud, and heard the horse-laugh of a host of city apprentices as I floundered out.'

Yet advertising for a wife was no longer confined solely to urban communities as, in a new development, the demographics of the personal columns began to broaden. The *Dorset County Chronicle* was founded in 1824, and eight years later a farmer named Charles Warren used it to look for a wife to help him take care not only of his three children, but also, crucially, of his pigs:

> My wife has been dead 12 months ago, last Shroton Fair: the children live with themselves in the day-time, but I am always at home with them at night. I do think that it would be better

if there was a woman to look after them, both for the children and myself. I have got 8s a week for my work, and the
boy 2s a week, and have constant employ. I want a good steady
woman, between 30 and 40 years old, for a wife. I do not want
a second family. I want a woman to look after the pigs while
I am out at work.

Warren is honest about the fact that in a rural community like
Marnhull, the Dorset village in which he lived, marriage was first
and foremost a business partnership, with the result that eligible
women wielded considerable power.

In 1841, nine years after the ad appeared, the census shows that
Warren, by now aged forty-five, was still living in Marnhull with
his three children, Robert, Hannah and Charles junior. There is no
sign of a wife. It is not until the census of 1871 that it is revealed
that Charles finally got remarried to a woman named Louisa, who
was thirty years younger than him. So perhaps the story does have
a happy ending after all.

Ads from working-class men like Warren were still hugely in the
minority (ads cost money, after all), but they tended to receive a
disproportionate amount of publicity, getting reprinted in the
national press and subjected to vicious mockery. For example, in
1838, *The Times* featured an ad from the *Gloucestershire Chronicle*, the
spelling and grammar of which left something to be desired, under
the sneering headline 'Matrimony and the March of Intellect'. Such
ads contributed to the continued perception that 'He, indeed, who
can descend to publish his wishes in this manner must be either a
knave or a fool', in the words of the *Leeds Mercury*.

Yet, in reality, most were simply lonely, respectable, middle-class
men who found themselves unlucky in love and refused to let the
taint of the Corder case deter them from turning to the newspapers for help. Taking a selection of ads between 1830 and 1860,
the advertisers range in profession from a commander in the merchant

services and a pharmaceutical chemist to an officer in the Bengal army and a tradesman 'in the Fancy Drapery line'. Occasionally an aristocrat popped up, causing a considerable splash and giving women everywhere renewed hope that Lonely Hearts ads really did offer the opportunity to marry up. In 1840 a Munich newspaper featured an ad, which was then widely reprinted in the British press, from seventy-year-old Baron von Hallberg de Broech, who sought to share his castle in Bavaria with some lucky girl: 'She whom I would wed must be from 16 to 20 years of age, she must have beautiful hair, handsome teeth and a charming little foot . . .' It was reported that he received a total of 749 replies: 'But he burnt them all and chose a wife who he does not reveal', except to say that she was the 'perfect woman' – charming foot and all, presumably.

To the average nineteenth-century British gentleman, image and reputation were everything: 'after his purse, nothing is more precious to [him] than his mask – the reputation he has managed to acquire', as the French activist Flora Tristan wrote in 1840. Modesty was no longer valued as a virtue in the way it once was. Hence, in 1841, a Lonely Hearts ad appeared in a London newspaper from 'A Barrister, only 28 years of age' who 'moves in the first circles, is a constant attendant at Court, and can give references to Noblemen and Judges of the land. He has taken the degree of Master of Arts at one of the Universities, made the grand tour of Europe, and was presented at nearly all the Foreign Courts'. Another gentleman, in 1844, describes himself as 'endowed with great personal attractions (reckoned very like Prince Albert) and who is also remarkable for his amiable and affectionate disposition . . .' Most Lonely Hearts ads are replete with exaggeration to some extent, but in this period the tendency was particularly encouraged by a general climate of puffery, more potent and prevalent than ever before. Here is John Stuart Mill on the subject: '. . . any voice, not pitched in an exaggerated key, is lost in the hubbub. Success, in so crowded a field, depends not upon what a person is, but upon what he seems . . .' A writer for *Blackwood's Magazine* identified this early on, bemoaning the way that Lonely Hearts ads had in recent years 'aimed too much at eloquence, they have rivalled too ardently the Packwood razor-strop and the Warren's liquid blacking style', while a letter to the *Leeds Mercury* in 1864 railed at length against 'these puffs for adventurers in the lottery of marriage'.

Not everyone got away with this sort of behaviour. That same year, one gentleman, having presented himself in even more rapturous terms than the usual matrimonial adventurer and then demanded that prospective candidates send him their *cartes* as 'other matters being equal, personal attractions would decide his choice', received the following tart reply: 'Sir, – I do not enclose my carte, for, though there is some authority for putting a cart before a horse, I know of none for putting one before an ass.'

Ads reveal much about the qualities that the perfect mid-nineteenth-century wife was meant to possess. Certain familiar adjectives crop up repeatedly – 'agreeable', 'affectionate' and 'respectable' – just as they did in the previous century. The ideal age continued to be between twenty and thirty. There was still no mention of sex, with the wording of Lonely Hearts ads remaining universally chaste right until the end of the twentieth century, existing in a kind of parallel universe where marriage and sex were presented as two entirely separate entities, in no way connected.

Also unchanging was the way that money, ideally plenty of it, continued to be a crucial factor. And this was, as ever, a matter for mockery – even in a remote parsonage in west Yorkshire. The drawing-room at the Brontë family home was regularly strewn with newspapers and magazines. Reverend Patrick Brontë took both the *Leeds Mercury* and the *Leeds Intelligencer*, and also had subscriptions to *Blackwood's Magazine* and *Fraser's Magazine*. Articles about Lonely Hearts ads (mostly reports of scandals, but occasionally success stories or opinion pieces) appeared in all of them from time to time, and thus the Reverend's eldest daughter Charlotte would have had plenty of opportunity to educate herself on the subject. And so it was that in the spring of 1839 Charlotte wrote a short story entitled 'Henry Hastings' that opens with a searing parody of the genre:

> A young man of captivating exterior, elegant address and most gentlemanlike deportment, is desirous of getting his bread easy & of living in the greatest possible enjoyment of comfort & splendour – at the least possible expense of labour and drudgery . . . The advertiser is not particular as to age – nor does he lay any stress on those fleeting charms of a merely personal nature . . . On the contrary, an imperfect symmetry of form – a limb – laterally – horizontally or obliquely bent aside from the line of rigid rectitude, or even the absence of a feature – as an eye too few, or a row of teeth minus – will be no material objection to this enlightened and sincere individual – provided only satisfactory testimonials be given of the possession of that one great & paramount virtue – that eminent & irresistible charm C-A-S-H!

At the very moment that Charlotte was writing 'Henry Hastings', she herself received a proposal of marriage from the Reverend Henry Nussey, who was the brother of a friend of hers, so she had matters of this sort on her mind. (One wonders what Charlotte's own Lonely Hearts ad might have said, had she ever felt moved to write one.)

Charlotte turned Nussey down. She goes on to describe the sort of wife she believes would suit him, almost as if she is composing a Lonely Hearts ad for him: 'Her character should not be too marked, ardent and original – her temper should be mild, her piety undoubted, her spirits even and cheerful, and her "personal attractions" sufficient to please your eye and gratify your just pride.' It was an astute assessment of what a typical early Victorian man sought in a wife. Other ads provide evidence that those who were 'lady-like', 'attractive' and 'domesticated' (which makes the prospective wife sound like a pet) also came to be highly prized, suggesting a new-found emphasis not only on outward appearance, but also on the home. Other popular qualities included 'religious' or 'pious', for this was an era of religious revival, with religion playing a more central role in everyday life than at any time since Puritanism had gripped the nation.

Ads began to appear like the one from a gentleman in search of a woman who 'could render him as perfectly happy in the nuptial state, as it will be his anxious wish to make her ... it shall be his constant and principal study to make her the happiest of women'. This was *the* era of companionate marriage. It became acceptable, normal even, for both men and women to aspire to reconcile making a strategic, dutiful marriage with the attainment of romantic love. Queen Victoria and Prince Albert were the perfect role models in this respect. Consciously encouraged by many Victorian commentators, the hope was that it would help strengthen the bonds of marriage by making it an emotional partnership as well as a practical one.

Victoria and Albert etching together in the 1840s. By G. Durand

There was also a nascent trend towards a more creative style of ad. One that appeared in the Birmingham newspaper *Aris's Gazette* in 1828 employed a sustained metaphor throughout, seeking a female 'companion' who was 'published earlier than 1790, either a first or second-hand, provided it is in good binding, and has gilt edges, with the contents in good keeping. Any Lady having such a treasure to dispose of will meet with a most devoted, attentive, secret reader ...' The implication is that the advertiser would like a wife who is interested in books. This idea that shared interests could be a factor in a successful relationship was new, but from the 1830s onwards it became increasingly common to stipulate that the successful candidate must like reading or 'have a taste for music'.

Yet those who tried to circumvent the traditional courtship system often suffered for their efforts. In the first half of the century hoaxes still tended to be in the Georgian mould – that is, they were almost always directed at men and purely for fun. Most follow a strikingly similar pattern: a man places an ad and a group of wags reply to it in the guise of a rich, genteel young lady. A tryst is arranged, but, when the advertiser arrives at the appointed location, the 'lady' is quickly revealed to be not at all the sort of person he had been led to expect. It was one of *the* jokes of the early Victorian period, endlessly hilarious, repeated over and over again in every corner of the country, and each time reported with undisguised glee in the national press.

On occasion the lady in question turned out to be 'an old and ugly woman, selected from the back quarters of Saffron-hill', as *The Times* reported of one hoax in 1830. At other times, she was a man in drag. In 1837 a group of pupils from Harrow school answered a Lonely Hearts ad pretending to be an eligible young lady. An arrangement was made to meet the hopeful gentleman in the local churchyard, where the couple would proceed to central London to watch the newly crowned Queen Victoria process through the streets of the capital for the very first time. At the appointed time 'a showilydressed female might be seen wending her way up the churchyard'. Her intended then also appeared, and off they went arm in arm. However, when they stopped at the nearby King's Head pub for refreshments,

> [their] arrival at this place was the signal for a general outbreak of mingled hisses, laughter and shouting, and the astounded wight, on turning to his fair companion to seek an explanation, was most ineffably horrified by seeing her pick up her petticoats under her arms and mizzle through the crowd, which immediately closed up and effectually covered her retreat. Soon afterwards one of the schoolboys, named Jervais, and vaguely resembling the false fair one, was noticed as being particularly active in the tumult.

The poor swain was rescued only by the arrival of the mathematics master.

By 1860 there were twenty-seven newspapers in existence outside London, in addition to forty-eight in the capital, six of which were published daily. Mass-circulation Sunday papers also became available, including the *News of the World, Lloyd's Weekly Newspaper* and *Reynolds's Newspaper*. These were printed on rag paper and were physically very tough, so that the same edition could be passed around and read by a number of different people. For the city dweller, they provided a filter for what was becoming an increasingly scary and confusing world; for women in particular, most of whom were largely confined to the home, they really did provide a window onto the world. W.H. Smith opened his first railway news-stand in 1848 at Euston station, based on the premise that railway travellers were a captive market of readers, delighted to be offered something to read during their journey. Add to this the abolition of newspaper tax in 1855 and the repeal of paper duty in 1861, and the result was a dramatic increase in the size and power of the British press. There were more newspapers and magazines than ever before, each one a potential site for a Lonely Hearts ad.

Many publications, however, refused to accept Lonely Hearts; in fact many did not accept ads of any sort, at least initially. Ads were judged to be full of untruths and lacking in respectability, and hence were uncommon in the middle-class press until a number of forces – the prospect of serious financial gain, the increasing purchasing power of the middle class and hence pressure on the newspapers from advertisers, and new techniques of illustration – combined to overcome resistance, and before long their pages were cluttered up with announcements for new cleaning products and miracle cures. 'Ads are spreading all over England,' according to *Punch* in 1847. '[T]hey have crept under the bridges – have planted themselves right in the middle of the Thames – have usurped the greatest thoroughfares – and are now just on the point of invading the omnibuses. Advertising is certainly the great vehicle for the age.' And the data bears this out: the total number of advertisements quadrupled between 1800 and 1848. They were further encouraged in 1857 when the *Daily Telegraph* invented the box-number system for classified advertisements, thereby securing the privacy of all those involved.

Lonely Hearts ads refused to fade away. This is perhaps surprising in view of cautionary tales like the one that appeared in the *Leeds Mercury* about 'An unlucky man, who, in order to get a family by a deceased wife taken care of, had been induced to marry a worthless drunken woman, through the medium of a matrimonial advertisement . . . [He] applied last week at Union Hall for advice, but, of course, nothing could be done for him.' It was, however, the stories of successful couplings that drew most attention from the press. In 1857, much was made of the Tyneside man who had advertised for a wife in a Midlands newspaper, gone on 'a tour of inspection' of a selection of the fifty to sixty women who replied, and ended up marrying one 'with whom he fell in love, at first sight'. No wonder those of a romantic bent continued to hope that they might have similar luck. 'We have been struck with the increase of matrimonial advertisements in the London, and some of the provincial newspapers,' commented *Reynolds's Newspaper* that same year.

'After this, good people, buy your wives and husbands at the livery establishments, as you would horses, dogs, etc. No more courting, flirting, bother, disappointment and wounded feelings. Step up to the office, examine the stock, take your pick, pay your money and drive to the parson. Hurrah for progress!' This was the magazine *Vanity Fair*'s sarcastic analysis in 1860, and it was true that even the matter of marriage was increasingly implicated in, and incorporated into Victorian Britain's pervasive culture of commerce. There was now an ad to suit almost everyone, whatever his or her predilections. One in the *Shoreditch Observer* in 1863 stated its case in the simplest of terms: 'Marriage. The advertiser wishes to meet with a young woman who has but one leg.'

Chapter Eight

The Tomfoolery of Silly Girls

ADA MILNE'S WEDDING day – 11 October 1882 – dawned bright and sunny. Ada had first met her intended when he answered the ad she had placed in one of the many newspapers that had sprung up over the course of the previous decade that were dedicated solely to matchmaking. This was her second shot at matrimonial bliss: her first, at the age of twenty-six, with a clerk named Edward Chippendale Milne (who, like her, was from Lancashire and hence probably a local match), had been blighted by her periodic stays in a Hertfordshire lunatic asylum. When he died in 1873, she moved to Tunbridge Wells. Widowhood did not suit her, however, and so Ada decided to insert an ad in the *Matrimonial News*. She was forty-four.

The ad, in which Ada announced to the world that she was a widow with £18,000 a year in search of a husband, was quickly spotted by one Edmund Binns, a thirty-five-year-old solicitor living in the suburbs of Sheffield with his elderly mother and unemployed sister. He replied, and after exchanging a few letters he arranged to travel down to Tunbridge Wells to meet Ada. However, when he arrived at her house, he was intercepted by her brother, John Liebert. Liebert was furious: his sister was in no position to make her own decisions, he told Edmund, since she had only recently been released from yet another lunatic asylum. And with that, he literally threw Edmund out.

But the new couple refused to be thwarted. A few weeks later Ada managed to get herself to Sheffield by train, where she and Edmund were reunited. He immediately asked her to marry him, and she agreed. When the vicar at Edmund's local Catholic church raised questions about the bride-to-be's mental state, Edmund produced three medical certificates, all of which certified her sanity. Thus the vicar had no choice but to consent to the ceremony.

The bride's brother, however, thought otherwise. He raced up to Sheffield and arranged for some local thugs to be waiting outside the church, ready to bundle Ada into a waiting carriage and whisk her away. At the same time, Edmund had himself organised for some members of the local police force to be in attendance, ostensibly in order to keep the peace. Hence when the bride arrived, her brother found himself being physically restrained by a policeman so that she might enter the church without an altercation.

The wedding began, and when the guests were asked whether they had any objection to the marriage, Mr Liebert shouted out in an attempt to convince the congregation that his sister was not of sound mind. But he had no proof, and so the ceremony continued and the couple were married. 'Mr Liebert was very much affected, and leant his head on one of the pews, weeping bitterly,' reported *The Times*.

The *Matrimonial News*, where Ada's ad had originally appeared, was the first newspaper ever to specialise in Lonely Hearts ads. 'Civilization, combined with the cold formalities of society and the rules of etiquette, imposes such restrictions on the sexes, that there are thousands of marriageable men and women, of all ages, capable of making each other happy, who never have a chance of meeting' was how it justified its existence in its launch issue, which went on sale on 19 April 1870. Placing an ad cost sixpence for forty words. This encouraged advertisers to be concise, generally relying on culturally accepted norms of what was deemed attractive: age, wealth, and so on. The result is a consistent and unique patterning of language, a little like the commercial variant of compressing a sonnet into fourteen lines. In terms of their background, however, the men and women featured – a land agent in Yorkshire, a colliery manager in Wales, a civil servant in India, a draper, a surgeon, a chemist and a governess – were so many and varied that the newspaper immediately received a stream of letters demanding to know whether they were genuine. '[A]ll the Notices in last Number were bona fide,' responded the editor the following week.

But the *Matrimonial News* did not monopolise the Lonely Hearts market for long. In 1871 the *Marriage Gazette* was founded, followed three years later by the *Matrimonial Times*. In total, the period between 1870 and 1900 saw the launch of no fewer than twenty weekly or monthly newspapers made up entirely of Lonely Hearts ads (in addition to a further seven covering all matters marriage-related). It is an astonishing figure, and indicative of the fact that, in the late-Victorian period, Lonely Hearts ads were more widespread and more popular than at any time up until Internet dating went mainstream in the 2000s.

The ads that appeared in these newspapers during the 1870s share a number of characteristics with those seen over the previous two centuries. There is the usual cavalcade of men in search of a wealthy wife to help extricate them from a financial catastrophe: the collapse of shares in gold on the New York Stock Exchange (also known as the Panic of 1869), say, or an unsuccessful mining venture.

An English gentleman, aged 60, with a little property, value £1000, he has no more, having lost £5000 by the panic. Will any lady have compassion on him, and settle down 'snug'. He has a rare and novel collection of antique and curious watches (42), cost between £500 and £600. Will any lady lend temporary £250 to establish a home in beautiful Normandy, and she to have the preference to possess it; write to Editor, with 4 stamps.
(*Matrimonial News*, 18 June 1870)

An English Gentleman, a widower (Protestant), age 33, height 5ft 9½ inches, was only married eleven months, is of a kind, cheerful disposition, dark complexion, well connected, gentlemanly in demeanour, extensively travelled, fond of prose and poetry, and passionately so of music, fond of children, and the domestic world or home, and believes he possesses all the qualifications a lady could reasonably expect in a gentleman, who, being mortal, is not quite an angel, he wishes to correspond with a lady of similar disposition, with the view to an early marriage. The lady would be required to have means to enable him to start in business, or otherwise as she might wish; he would insure his life, and settle all on herself; he lost his fortune by the failure of mining speculation, and is now residing with his parents, who are in extensive business, which will fall to him.
(*Matrimonial News*, 2 January 1875)

Having been burnt so badly by economic speculation, one might think these men would have been wary of indulging in romantic speculation too, but apparently not. Other, more personal sob stories also reveal themselves, for example, the 'English gentleman, practising abroad as civil and consulting engineer and architect, 33', who '[w]ishes to correspond with a lady of moderate means, who would not object to live abroad, good society, but where little English is spoken, as the advertiser has already suffered ruin, shame, and pity, as the result of a seven years misalliance'.

In other respects, however, the ads differ considerably from their earlier counterparts. One placed in the *Matrimonial News* in 1875 by a thirty-year-old lawyer who, 'weary of leading single life, wishes to meet a Venus who could love an Adonis', anticipates the more idiosyncratic style of language that tends to characterise today's ads. There was also a rise in the number of men looking for a wife willing to live abroad: 'become a Bonanzo queen,' exhorts one. From the Wild West to India, increased travel to America and the opening up of Britain's colonies offered a whole new world of opportunities for women in search of adventure.

Most significantly of all, in the 1870s ads from women began to appear again, following a more than half-century absence from the classified pages. Here are just a few that appeared in the *Matrimonial News* during its first year:

> Lena, the daughter of a professional gentleman, is between 30 and 40 years of age, not tall, dark hair, pleasant countenance, and possesses a warm loving disposition, but owing to a trial early in life, has only now concluded it is best to marry, as she, like the ivy, requires some thing to cling to and fill up the void in her heart. Editor has Lena's address.
>
> (10 September 1870)

> A young lady, aged 22, the orphan daughter of a country gentleman, of old family, would like to marry. She is well-educated, accustomed to good society, and has travelled much; is a capital housekeeper; can ride, and drive a pair; is musical, and dresses exquisitely, and wants some one awfully jolly. No clergymen, doctors, or learned men need apply, but an easy-going kind of fellow, with a fairish amount of brains, would suit admirably. Editor has address.
>
> (29 October 1870)

> Daisy, a young lady, authoress and composer in music, wishes to meet with a true English gent with a view to marriage, from 28 to 33 years of age. Daisy is 25, is accomplished, talented, and has a great love for nature, appreciates all that is beautiful and worthy of admiration. She is medium in height, and complexion, has brown hair, and blue eyes, and has a v affectionate disposition, but alas! does not possess the great BAIT,

MONEY. If any gentleman thinks she would be a suitable partner, cartes would be exchanged, as Editor has address.
   (10 December 1870)

Whether the voice heard is that of a struggling authoress, a penniless orphan or a woman like Lena who, 'like the ivy, requires something to cling to and fill up the void in her heart', all indicate a brave attempt to try to take control of their own destiny. Middle-class women were the impetus behind the spread of ads during this period. An article in the *Pall Mall Gazette* in 1871 quoted an ad in the *Manchester Examiner* from 'Blanche and Lily' – 'Two young ladies of education (Sisters), aged twenty and twenty-four, with small incomes, would correspond with two young gentlemen with a view to matrimony' – and went on to marvel at the huge number of ads that had recently appeared in the Manchester press: 'Few people have the slightest notion of the yearning for affection which prevails in the manufacturing districts.'

The trouble was that time was not on the side of women like 'Blanche' and 'Lily'. Mary Paley Marshall noted that, in the 1860s, 'the notion was common that if a girl did not marry or at any rate become engaged by twenty she was not likely to marry at all'. Accordingly, contemporary conduct literature decreed that, for women, the ideal age for a wedding to occur was between twenty and twenty-five. Yet eliciting a marriage proposal was not easy, and was made even more challenging by one of the revelations contained in the census of 1861: Britain was experiencing a significant numerical surplus of women, the result of young men emigrating more and dying younger. Women were not 'some rare, unattainable thing, seldom met with – rarely seen', noted the *Leeds Mercury* in 1864. Quite the opposite: 'to take a commercial view of the case, owners are overpowered with stock in hand'. What emerged from this was a profound fear of spinsterhood, even among women only just out of their teens: 'Lilian, Gladys and Rosalie, daughters of a deceased officer, have good incomes, ages 22, 20 and 18, don't wish to die old maids. Ride and drive as only Irish ladies can.'

The fact that women like 'Lilian, Gladys and Rosalie' had the means to advertise in a paper like the *Matrimonial News* is evidence of the burgeoning purchasing power of the Victorian middle class. Between 1850 and 1870, the average middle-class income rose by approximately £100 per person, and opportunities to spend this extra cash increased accordingly. There were rumblings of a retail revolution, beginning with the opening of the first department stores. A trip to Whiteley's in west London, for example, was an excuse for 'Lilian, Gladys and Rosalie' to have a day out in town without a chaperone, thereby not only escaping the confinement of the fireside, but also establishing a public identity for themselves. Some historians have argued that the very act of choosing a product from the department store's shelves helped women learn to express their needs and expand their horizons. Taken together, these developments meant that shopping – whether for hats or for men – became easier and more enjoyable for women than ever before.

Whiteley's department store in Bayswater in 1900

The launch of so many matrimonial newspapers in the 1870s was duly noted in the mainstream press. '[M]arriage by advertisement [is] a natural result of our fondness for machinery' was how the *Daily News* explained the phenomenon in 1877. 'As advertisements of this sort do not die a natural death, the melancholy certainty is forced on one, that a great many people are coarse in their tastes, and will do anything for a poor joke or a dubious flirtation.' It is a familiar attempt to deny the genuine need of many of those who advertised, to which end some even tried to get the issue raised in Parliament. An ad in a national newspaper in 1878 from a widowed vicar – 'thirty-nine, 5ft 9in, considered good-looking' – prompted a journalist for the *Pall Mall Gazette* to comment, 'Let us hope that it will be shown up in Parliament as it deserves, and that it may have, at all events, the salutary effect of accelerating the suppression of this disgraceful traffic in the cure of souls . . .'

'[N]ot a pleasing product of our latest civilization,' was the *Pall Mall Gazette*'s final judgement. Nonetheless, the ads kept on coming, with the launch of the *Matrimonial Record* (1882), *Matrimonial Herald* (1884), *Aristocratic Matrimonial & Marriage Envoy* (1884), *Marriage Advertiser* (1886) and *Cupid's Cosmopolitan Carrier* (1888), which was printed in English and French and styled itself as pan-European: 'A young Russian nobleman, prepossessing and considered handsome, of a well-known family, Aide-de-camp and Lieutenant in the Imperial Guard at St Petersburg, Protestant, would marry an accomplished young lady with fortune of her own.'

The *Matrimonial Herald* was the most popular of all of these, with the first edition setting out some of the reasons why the need for it was so great: 'The cold formalities and the exclusiveness of modern society, the reserve of character of the people composing it, the diffidence of those who feel that their experience and cultivation do not befit them to mix in it . . .' It then gave three examples of the sort of person it hoped would benefit from the service it offered. First was 'the successful commercial man, who hesitates to enter the

portals of fashion and expose his crudeness and unpolish in a sphere
of culture, refinement, and *bon ton* . . .' Then there was 'the recluse,
who perhaps, by a long course of study, has warped those bright
qualifications of character which makes a man popular in society
. . .' Finally, there was 'the maiden, who being characterized by the
most sterling and deep qualities of mind, is not calculated to appear
so favourably in fashionable and brilliant gatherings as her more
vivacious and superficial sisters . . .' It was not only an attempt to
flatter readers into entrusting the newspaper with their hearts (and
their purses), but was also a pitch at the level of clientele – prosperous businessmen, well-brought-up young ladies – that it hoped
to attract.

Following a very successful first few months, during which the
number of ads submitted to its pages increased enormously, the
Matrimonial Herald triumphantly bandied the rallying cry that 'a revolution is taking place!'. It compared the rise of matrimonial
newspapers to Robert Stephenson's invention of the *Rocket*, the world's
first modern locomotive: 'Steam, the greatest invention of the age,
met with the most determined and inveterate opposition from all
classes of the public, and it was only by the obstinate persistency
of the constructor of the "Rocket" that our present lightning mode
of transit became an accomplished fact . . . The *Matrimonial Herald*
is a typical "Rocket".'

A large number of those who advertised in the *Matrimonial Herald*
in 1884 were drawn, as usual, from the middle class: lawyers, archi-
tects, bankers, a parliamentary reporter, a retired Lancashire mill
owner, a curate, an accountant and 'a young literary gent whose writ-
ings have already caused considerable sensation in the literary world'.
A new development, however, was the number of working-class men
and women who featured in its pages. They included two engine
drivers on the Indian railways, a shoe-maker, a wood engraver, a
baker, a gas fitter, a furniture-maker, a railway signalman, a market
gardener, a brass finisher, a harness-maker, a carpenter, a telegraph

Men and women at work making Valentine's Day cards. Were they also dreaming of receiving one themselves?

clerk, a mechanic and a draper in Peckham. Among the women there were numerous domestic servants – even 'A Superior Domestic', which is how one of them tried to sell herself – a lady's maid, a bookkeeper, a shop assistant in a West End drapery and another in the hat department of a West End department store. It is not impossible that some of these were fabricated in order to drum up business; nonetheless, they are indicative of the expanded customer base at which, a few issues in, the *Matrimonial Herald* was aimed.

This increased proportion of ads from working-class men and women was found in all the matrimonial newspapers of the 1880s, even including the *Aristocratic Matrimonial & Marriage Envoy*, despite its highfalutin title. It was in part stimulated by rising literacy rates, which, combined with the falling price of newspapers, meant that these publications came within reach of the masses for the very first time. A more significant stimulus, however, was demand. Marriage rates among the working class shot up during the last three decades of the nineteenth century. In response to decades of moral campaigning, expressions of sexual non-conformity such as common-law marriage were becoming less acceptable. The New Poor Law of 1834, which decreed that an unmarried mother no longer had a right to relief from the state unless she agreed to enter a workhouse, also encouraged many to tie the knot.

Widespread economic uncertainty meant that there was a greater need than ever for working-class men and women to join forces. Britain in the 1880s was in the middle of an economic downturn, the result of a combination of factors including a series of disastrous harvests, competition from foreign imports (particularly wheat) and labour unrest. In addition, the continuing evolution of industrial capitalism meant that many of the trades that had previously employed women (such as textiles) were in decline, with the result that the number of women in paid employment steadily decreased in the later years of the nineteenth century and a new family set-up emerged, in which the man was the main breadwinner and the woman stayed at home. The options available to women outside marriage remained severely limited. 'Better a bad husband than no husband at all,' a neighbour in Flora Thompson's village retorted when a young Flora announced that she had no intention of ever settling down. Street ballads and penny romances also encouraged many a young woman to yearn for a knight in shining armour to come and whisk her away from life's daily grind.

But how was a girl supposed to find her knight? Research has revealed that, among the working class, 42 per cent of couples met through friends, neighbours or relations, 27 per cent became acquainted at work, 14 per cent were introduced at group events like a party or a church service and 6 per cent initially had a landlord-tenant relationship; 11 per cent, however, met in some random fashion that was entirely outside the control of the community – a Lonely Hearts ad, a matchmaker or, most commonly, in the street. This is supported by accounts given to the nurses at the Thomas Coram Foundling Hospital of the circumstances in which the mothers had first encountered the fathers of the illegitimate children they were about to leave there: 'I first met the Father in the street as I went to the public house for beer'; 'He was a policeman on duty in the square, and used to speak to me'; 'I met him when I was going to my place and he helped me with my box.' With the young leaving home earlier than ever before in search of employment, Britain's cities thronged with men barely out of their teens, hunting for romantic assignations. Women were picked up in the street or in the pub, in museums and parks and music halls, on trains or even at church. For many, therefore, meeting a partner continued to be very much a matter of chance.

In 1885, the city of Bristol became the proud home of the *Matrimonial Post*, the only matrimonial newspaper to be based outside London. It was an instant hit and ran for sixty years, the longest of any of them. By 1888, according to the *Pall Mall Gazette*,

Ice rinks were a popular *rendez-vous* for courting couples (*Punch,* 1876)

'matrimonial journals have really not only been acclimatized in this
country, but have a tangible *raison d'etre* and a sufficiently successful
business on their hands'. The last decade of the century also saw
the launch of the *Matrimonial Chronicle* (1890), *Matrimonial World* (1891),
Matrimonial Courier (1891), *Honeymoon* (1891), *Matrimonial Times* (1891,
the title's second incarnation), *Matrimonial Intelligencer* (1896) and
Matrimonial Register (1896).

The women who advertised in the 1890s were predominantly
either working-class or miserable. In the first edition alone of the
newly relaunched *Matrimonial Times,* one finds 'A young Jewess (an
orphan) wishing to get away from her friends and relatives, who
keep her (much against her will) very secluded', 'A Lady, 38 years
of age, who has lived in India several years, and has lately returned
home through the death of her father'; and 'A Maiden Lady, of
middle age [who] has had many cares and worries during her life'.
(One can only speculate what those 'cares and worries' might be.)
Of the men, a significant proportion worked in the colonies, such

as the 'English Gentleman, in India, holding a Government appointment of £300 a year, with good prospects, tall, fair, cheerful disposition, age 28'.

Also noticeable is the increasing appearance of the phrase, 'Photos exchanged'. It had been in occasional use since the invention of the *carte de visite* in 1854, but in 1888 the first easy-to-use camera, the Kodak, was launched ('You press the button, we do the rest'), with the result that people no longer had to make a special trip to a photography studio to obtain a portrait of themselves. A report in *The Sun* in 1893 by its founder and editor T.P. O'Connor revealed that, of the 300 applications a fortnight that the *Matrimonial News* received, most included a photograph: 'a somewhat prim-looking maiden of uncertain age, but in possession of a good fortune, was depicted imbibing a cup of afternoon tea; a young French actress looked very bright and chic, muffled up in an opera cloak; whilst a stout German girl had forwarded her likeness with a view to inducing an Englishman to fetch her from the Fatherland'. Fairly or unfairly, physical appearance now played a role right at the beginning of any courtship initiated through a newspaper.

In 1888, an investigative journalist at the *Pall Mall Gazette* revealed that it was common for a matrimonial newspaper to double as a marriage agency. London alone had ten of them, each of which spent between £5 and £10 a day on advertising. The likes of the *Matrimonial Herald, Post* and *Times* therefore contributed significantly to the revenue of many a provincial newspaper. The 18 March 1892 edition of the *Bristol Mercury*, for example, featured ads for both the *Herald* and the *Post*, in addition to ads that purported to have been placed by individuals (an orphaned young lady with £500 a year, another with savings of £8,000), but in reality were probably intended to drum up business for these same publications. However, the establishment in 1893 of the Society for Checking the Abuses of Public Advertising led to a tightening up of advertising regulations, and ads of this sort gradually disappeared from mainstream newspapers.

The beneficiaries? Specialist newspapers like those with the word 'matrimonial' in their title.

With more and more matrimonial newspapers competing for business, it was inevitable that some folded after just one year or even one issue. Others turned to ever more dubious methods to stay afloat. This was, after all, the age of 'New Journalism' when newspapers increasingly began to blur fact and fiction by, among other ploys, printing fabricated letters to the editor in an attempt to stir up controversy. The matrimonial newspapers were no different. Two ads that appeared next to each other in an edition of the *Matrimonial Post* seem to have been composed solely to pique interest: one was supposedly from a 'Foreign Prince, with large landed estates in North and South America and the West Indies', the other from 'A pretty and attractive young Lady, age 17, with fair hair, blue eyes, and a full figure . . . will have £350 a year in her own right on attaining her eighteenth year.' This description of a blue-eyed, blonde, seventeen-year-old heiress with 'a full figure' appeals perfectly to many men's fantasy of the perfect wife. No wonder the *Post*'s editor felt compelled to defend himself from accusations of deception: 'surprise is frequently expressed at the *very large number* of ads . . . and in not a few instances doubts have been uttered as to the genuineness of their particulars. What it may be with other agencies we do not pretend to say – we hold ourselves completely aloof from and quite above any *packing* . . .' (that is, from filling the pages with made-up ads).

'The original and only trust-worthy paper': so read the masthead of the *Matrimonial News*, which claimed to have facilitated 'thousands' of marriages. By the 1890s, however, it too was fabricating a significant proportion of its ads. The June 1891 edition alone is crowded with men and women who are surely too good to be true. They include 'A Lady, 44, tall, fair and handsome with £3000 a year' named Fanny Fair; a 'Gentleman between 60 and 70, tall and good-looking, with nice residence and 2000l. a year' named Charlie Chesterfield;

a 'Handsome young Widow, aged 30, and large means' named Nellie Lovelace; and 'A Nobleman, of good means, age 40' named Lord George G. The preponderance on the newspaper's pages of blonde, moneyed women and aristocratic, moneyed men must have aroused suspicion, if nothing else. Furthermore, not only do none of the names proffered – Fanny Fair, Charlie Chesterfield – match up in public records even roughly with the ages they give, but they also sound far too similar to characters in a Victorian music-hall skit to be genuine. While it may be that the *News*'s readers assumed they were pseudonyms, their regular use nonetheless diminished the aura of respectability that the newspaper worked so hard to project.

In 1890, the *Matrimonial News* suffered a serious blow when it found itself at the centre of a national scandal. The owner and editor, Leslie Fraser Duncan, was sued for breach-of-promise. This was by no means the first breach-of-promise case to arise out of a Lonely Hearts ad, but it was the first to receive a significant amount of attention in the national press, primarily due to the fact that the plaintiff, twenty-one-year-old Gladys Knowles, had aristocratic connections. She was the granddaughter of Sir Francis Knowles and the niece of Admiral Knowles; her father was dead and she lived alone with her mother in Fulham.

Miss Knowles first visited the Oxford Street offices of the *Matrimonial News* in March 1889 – 'for the fun of it' and 'to see what it was', or so she later claimed in court. She was ushered into Mr Duncan's office, and they had a long chat. A few days later she went to see him again, this time accompanied by her mother, at which point Mr Duncan made a startling suggestion: he would like to marry Miss Knowles himself.

Miss Knowles was delighted. Mr Duncan became a regular visitor to the Knowles's house in Fulham and on 2 April during a carriage ride around Richmond Park, he officially proposed marriage. He was 'mad about her', he said. When Miss Knowles accepted, he gushed that he wanted the wedding to take place as soon as possible.

Within days, however, he began to detail a cavalcade of spurious reasons why the wedding might have to be delayed. Nonetheless, the couple continued to exchange love letters and he soon persuaded her to come down to his country house in Ham for the weekend, with the assurance that his elderly housekeeper would act as a chaperone. He also requested that she bring a wedding dress 'just in case', telling her that the local vicar was a friend of his. The visit passed 'without any impropriety', but Mr Duncan continued to stall about the wedding: the vicar was away, apparently, and he 'feared the curate would laugh at him on account of his age'.

A few weeks later Miss Knowles was again enticed to go and stay in Ham, this time without her mother's knowledge and without the presence of the housekeeper. On the Sunday night, she retired to bed at about eleven o'clock, making sure to lock her bedroom door, but later woke up to find Mr Duncan looming over her. 'Leave the room this instant!' she demanded. He grabbed her hand, a struggle ensued and she screamed, and the next thing she remembered was recovering consciousness, drenched in water. When she threatened to leave the house immediately, he pleaded with her: 'For God's sake don't do that or you'll ruin me.' She eventually agreed.

On Monday morning the two of them travelled up to London, ostensibly to apply for a marriage licence. She accompanied him to a hotel – 'of course, no woman of the world would have done so,' the judge later commented – where they were shown to a bed-sitting room. 'This is your room,' said Mr Duncan. 'I am going into the coffee room.' He left her alone, but an hour and a half later there was a knock at her door and there he was (in court Miss Knowles claimed that she only opened the door because she thought it was the chambermaid). 'This is my room, please go away,' she said. 'Nonsense,' he replied, 'it is my room too,' and forced his way in. She reminded him of his promise that they could have separate rooms. 'How foolish of you, when we are to be married in the morning,' he replied. 'If you don't leave off making this scene I won't marry you at all.' 'If you come near me, I'll scream,' she retorted. Mr Duncan swore violently at her and flung himself down on the bed, at which point she escaped downstairs to the hotel lobby where she sat until dawn broke. In the words of the judge, 'It was almost astonishing that the poor girl should have had firmness enough under such circumstances to resist him as she did.'

Throughout the summer months that followed, Mr Duncan continued to assure Miss Knowles that he planned to marry her tomorrow, next weekend, next month, next year. In an attempt to chivvy him along, she inserted a marriage announcement in the *Morning Post*, and at this point Duncan changed tactics. He suddenly claimed not only that he had recently lost a lot of money, but also that he had seven children by five different women to support and that his real age was sixty-nine, not sixty-three as he had previously claimed. When Miss Knowles threatened legal action, he wrote to her breaking off the engagement once and for all. A trial would, he declared, destroy her reputation: 'you will be obliged to admit your hotel adventure, and will never be able to show your face again'.

But Miss Knowles went ahead with the prosecution regardless. On 13 August 1890, as she rose from the witness box having finished giving evidence, she fainted and had to be carried from the courtroom. It took the jury less than half an hour to award her the staggeringly high figure of £10,000 in damages (though this was later reduced to £6,500). Yet for Miss Knowles, as the *Manchester Times* noted, 'there could be no restitution that was fully adequate'. Women such as her 'like what they believe to be the romance of exchanging photographs, of meeting and recognising one another by some flower or token; and if the man is unscrupulous the girl is soon entangled in a scandal from which she cannot break free. Perhaps the recent proceedings will stop the tomfoolery of silly girls, and lessen the extraordinary number of matrimonial advertisements.' The implication was that it was Miss Knowles who was to blame for what happened, not Mr Duncan, and *The Times* agreed: 'people who regard marriage as a matter of answering advertisements are not likely to be nice people'.

Miss Knowles, however, had the last laugh. A mere eight months after the trial, she married a twenty-nine-year-old Liverpudlian dentist named Alfred Prager and moved into a small but picturesque house in Marylebone. The *Matrimonial News* did not fare so well. In 1895, after twenty-five years of continuous publication, it finally folded.

That same year, another matrimonial newspaper, the *Matrimonial Herald*, was caught up in a scandal so outrageous that it made the Knowles–Duncan case appear trivial by comparison. The proprietors were charged with conspiring to obtain money under false pretences. It was a complicated case lasting more than four months that was covered breathlessly in the press, revealing as it did more than ever before about the secret workings of the matrimonial business.

The general gist of the prosecution's case was as follows: the *Herald* had been set up as a store-front for a marriage agency known as the World's Great Marriage Association. However, when applications to the Association proved scarce, the proprietors proceeded to place ads in provincial newspapers, first for the *Herald* and then, more deviously, for entirely fabricated individuals in search of a spouse. Anyone who replied was sent a copy of the Association's prospectus, along with a personalised letter that claimed the Association had the perfect match for them on its books. Those who agreed to pay the joining fee were then sent a list of prospective partners, most of whom were revealed in court to be fictitious. Almost all purported to be rich widows or orphans keen to marry in a hurry, and correspondence tended to be broken off after just one or sometimes two letters with the claim that the woman in question had moved to Egypt or the Riviera, or had met someone else, or died.

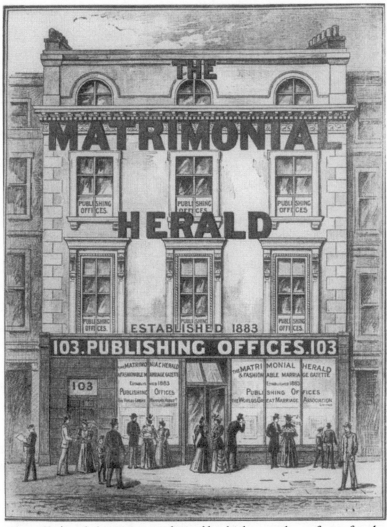

The offices of the *Matrimonial Herald*, which was also a front for the World's Great Marriage Association, on New Oxford Street in 1895

When police searched the offices of the Association, the index books revealed the names and addresses of more than 30,000 single men and women who had answered ads: one from a Mr Cecil received 357 replies, another from a Ms Hantly received 163. Also in the files were nearly 700 letters of thanks from satisfied customers, including one from an ex-Cabinet minister and one from a 'high-born' lady who had married the son of a peer. Yet, even though the police officer in charge of the search testified in court that he was certain these letters were genuine, it also turned out that Scotland Yard had been receiving complaints about the Association's operations for years. When this was put to John Charles Skates, one of the proprietors, during the raid, he protested that 'All these complaints have come from outsiders, who expected to secure a wife at once. We do a very extensive and legitimate business, and we have brought about marriage with very eminent persons', adding that on their books they had, among others, a judge and a foreign ambassador.

The trial opened on 12 November 1895. With few women willing to risk their reputation in court, the majority of the witnesses were men, and they came not only from London, but from all over the country (a house decorator in Yorkshire, a forester in Scotland), indicating the newspaper's extensive geographical reach. The first witness to be called by the prosecution was an electrician living in Westminster named Charles Otto. He testified that he had answered a Lonely Hearts ad in the *Echo*, as a result of which he was sent a copy of the *Matrimonial Herald* along with a letter offering him membership of the World's Great Marriage Association. He was then sent details of a Miss L. Burford: '24, blue eyes, brown hair, rather tall, accomplished, domesticated, £600'. Having written to her, he was informed she was no longer available but that, for a further fee, he could be introduced to a number of other women who were.

When Otto was cross-examined, the defence focused on what he had told the Association he was looking for in a wife.

'Your *sine qua non* was £1,000 a year in hard cash, wasn't it?'

'I made that a condition,' replied Otto.

'And what is your own value?'

'I have been earning £3 a week with Messrs. Siemens Brothers.'

'And what is your total value?'

'I have expectations.'

'Yes, of a rich marriage?'

'No; and I have a pound or two saved.'

'And when you wrote to these ladies you knew that you would soon be out of a job. Work was getting rather slack, wasn't it?'

'No, not that,' Otto protested. He was then questioned about his stated preference for an orphan.

'Oh, so you did not wish for a mother-in-law?' asked the defence.

'No,' said Otto, much to the amusement of the large crowd in the public gallery.

This exchange typified the way the defence team chose to approach the case. They ridiculed these lower- and lower-middle-class men on a number of levels. They were stupid to have fallen for the scam. They were pathetic for being so keen – desperate even – to get married. And they were greedy for hoping to snare a wife who was much richer than they were. It was a profoundly hypocritical attitude, when it was society urging them to get married in the first place, and furthermore to ensure any match was an advantageous one.

But these men's real crime was that they did not know their place. Hence, went the thinking, they were to be punished for their attempts at class transgression. The defence tried to present the whole affair as one big joke and, indeed, in summing up the case the judge noted how much laughter had been heard in the courtroom throughout the hearing. The newspaper coverage was equally snobbish in tone, taking great delight in encouraging its primarily middle-class readership to chuckle at the foolish antics of the working class.

Also called to the witness stand was George Bason, a short, bald, forty-four-year-old widower who had a four-year-old child and worked in a shoe factory in Northampton, where he earned twenty-four shillings a week. Bason had the misfortune to spot one of the Association's fake ads in the *Weekly Times and Echo*. Having been persuaded to pay the subscription fee, he informed it that he '[s]hould like a handsome young lady, widow, one with no family and with an independency in her own right to do as she liked with ... I know that some ladies don't like too mutch loving, but the lady must expect it from me – in fact, she must be all love ... I could not be happy with her money and not her love.' The defence made much of Bason's apparent lack of education, the implication being that it was not the Association's fault that it had failed to find him a wife. The cross-examination was so traumatic for Bason that at the end of it he fainted on the witness stand.

The press seized on this episode with glee. By fainting, Bason upheld the perception that any man who was willing – and even keen – to live off his wife, rather than earn his own living, must be somehow womanish. The implication was that no real man would even consider this sort of domestic set-up. According to one modern historian of the case, 'A new masculine identity was in the process of being constructed in the late nineteenth century', one where men were the sole breadwinners. Hence by ridiculing the victims' trangression of accepted gender roles first in the courtroom and then in the press, the trial was used 'to police both male courtship and notions of masculinity'. The fact that more of the victims were men than women meant it was viewed not as a tragedy, but as a farce.

Evidence was also heard from William G. Pitcher, a Blackfriars man living with his brother-in-law, who saw an ad in the *Norfolk News* supposedly from a Mrs Castle, but actually from the Association. 'And did you really think that you – 22 years of age, earning nothing, and with £40 capital only – could get a wife?' asked the defence. 'Yes, Sir,' replied Pitcher, going on to complain that most of the women the Association offered him were domestic servants with no money. 'That was not what I expected. I expected at least a thousand or two.' Others who testified included Henry Sutton, a clerk living in Bow who wanted a rich wife in order to be able 'to practice the flute as much as possible', and Alfred Jordan, a tobacconist with shops in both London and Brighton who claimed to be England's foremost draughts player. Having seen one of the Association's ads in the *People*, he sent them an extensive list of all the qualities he looked for in a wife: not only should she have an income of at least £200 a year, but she must also be

> able to see and hear without artificial aid, spinster, middle class, must be English and belong to the Church of England, and must be domestic, musical, well-educated, fond of tennis and games of skill and able to swim, should take an interest in sociology, temperance, dress reform, hygiene, &c., and if she would be able to interest herself in draughts, cricket or billiards so much the better.

Following testimony from a handwriting expert that the letters the Association forwarded to these men were in fact all written in the same hand, it did not take long for the jury to reach a verdict. John Charles Skates, the acknowledged ringleader, was sentenced to five years' penal servitude, while two of his cohorts each received three years. It was an exceedingly severe punishment, given the circumstances.

Just as guilty, however, in the eyes of the press and the public, were those poor souls who, by giving evidence, had laid themselves open to such severe humiliation. Newspapers in this period were fixated on depictions of bad behaviour, all the while thrusting issues of social and sexual decorum on to the public agenda. The *Matrimonial Herald* trial took place just six months after Oscar Wilde's conviction for sodomy, and was similarly a manifestation of the Victorian crusade for moral reform, which by the 1890s was nearing the heart of the political debate. The fact that lower- and lower-middle class men like Charles Otto and George Bason had the financial means to advertise for a wife contributed to the widespread sense of panic that it was exactly this sort of increased prosperity that would destroy society's moral fabric. Lonely Hearts ads were not only a public manifestation of vice, but – even more shockingly, in the view of some – they also blurred the line between the public and private, a line that was at the very heart of the Victorian moral code. The result was that the courts jumped at the chance to punish those who promoted them.

All that the men who fell for the *Matrimonial Herald*'s scams had forfeited was a few shillings and perhaps a little of their pride. Women, on the other hand, tended to be far more seriously affected when a liaison occasioned by a Lonely Hearts ad went awry. To reply to an ad was to make oneself vulnerable to exploitation by unscrupulous men and to risk serious damage to one's reputation. On 30 May 1893, the eyes of Hannah Tring, a widow with a five-year-old son living in Thornton Heath, fell upon the following ad:

> Matrimony. Civil servant, tall, fair, thirty; pay £150, Churchman, literary, energetic, wishes to meet young lady (or widow) with means or home. Address full particulars, with photo (returned), in confidence.

It turned out to have been placed by Charles Leman, a clerk in the secretary's department of the General Post Office living in East Dulwich. The two exchanged letters, and Lemen then visited Mrs Tring at her home and 'became intimate with her under the promise of marriage', as one newspaper delicately phrased it. On 27 February 1894, a baby girl was born. When Leman refused to take responsibility, Mrs Tring enlisted a friend, Mrs Thompson, to confront him. His response? 'I called a doctor. What more could I do?' Ignoring Leman's protests that Mrs Tring was 'loose' and that she had conspired with Mrs Thompson to bring charges, a court ordered him to pay 3s. 6d. a week until the child reached the age of fourteen, plus costs. Similar tales of a Lonely Hearts ad eventually resulting in an illegitimate child were being heard in courthouses up and down the country at around the same time.

Men like Leman were after sex; others, however, were after money. And while this was by no means a new phenomenon, the 1890s was the first time that those who attempted to use a Lonely Hearts ad to perpetrate financial fraud were routinely reported, tried and convicted in a public court of law. It is therefore possible to determine the scale of this particular crime during this period, and the numbers are shocking: there are scores and scores of them, and those are just the ones that made it to trial. This was after all *the* era of thieves, hustlers and con-artists – of 'white-collar crime'.

'Army pensioner, aged 35, good situation and pension, 100l. capital, would correspond with a lady. View, matrimony. No agents.' This ad, placed by a Peckham clerk named Horace Tulle in June 1899, was spotted by twenty-five-year-old Emma Grimwood, a pretty brunette with two beauty spots on her left cheek, who lived in Putney and worked as a cook. She wrote to him and he quickly replied, detailing how at the age of eighteen he had enlisted in the Royal Artillery, and had subsequently served in India and then Afghanistan, where he was wounded in the left knee and shoulder at the battle of Dargai. He claimed to live on a life pension of 2s. 6d. a day and asserted that he 'should like to settle down, as there is so little comfort in bachelor lodging'. This last line produced great laughter when it was read out in court.

The couple met for the first time outside the Royal Agricultural Hall in Islington. The courtship progressed rapidly, and by August a plan had emerged to get married and buy and run a coffee-house together in Penge. However, the moment Miss Grimwood lent her betrothed £20, he disappeared from her life entirely. On investigation, he was revealed to be a married man with a child and a string of aliases; the War Office had no knowledge of him, and certainly did not pay him a pension. Detectives at Scotland Yard had known about his fraudulent use of Lonely Hearts ads for nearly five years, but had been unable to find anyone willing to testify against him in court – that is, until the courageous Miss Grimwood came along. In her view, the reason he got away with it was because 'he was so very artful. His conduct and letters were so nice and gentlemanly – he never said or wrote a word that anyone could take objection to.' But, she continued, 'I can't say I ever loved him. I liked him, certainly, for his nice ways, and I suppose I should have gone on until love did come. A married friend of mine, who advised me in the matter, said "If you don't stick to a man like that, who is so attentive to you, you deserve never to get another one."'

Horace Tulle in the dock, from *Lloyd's Weekly Newspaper*, 15 October 1899

At least Miss Grimwood managed to escape Tulle's clutches before she got married to him. Others were not so lucky. In 1899, an ad appeared in the *Gloucestershire Echo*: 'Matrimony. Mechanic (32) wishes to correspond with domestic servant or widow with little means, view early marriage, write enclosing photo, in strict confidence, 30l. Echo office, Cheltenham.' The 'Mechanic' was Frederick Hall, who, over a number of years, 'practised a heartless system of deception on servant girls and other women', according to *The Times*.

Hall's *modus operandi* was to ensnare his victim via a Lonely Hearts ad, marry her, borrow money and jewellery from her, then disappear from her life for ever. He would then move on to the next. It worked at least six times before he was caught. Mary-Ann Dormer, a launderess from Caversham, replied to one of Hall's ads, married him within a week and they travelled to London together, paid for by Dormer. She also entrusted him with a ring, a watch and a chain 'for safe-keeping', as well as £11 in cash. About two weeks after their wedding, they were in a cab driving down Pentonville Road in Islington when Hall stopped the vehicle and asked her to get out and buy him some cigarettes. This she did, but when she turned around a moment later to ask Hall to get the cigarettes himself, he was nowhere to be seen. She waited for him for more than an hour before she realised she had been duped. When he was arrested, Hall remarked, 'I have had a pretty good innings and I must put up with it.' He pleaded guilty to bigamy, fraud and theft and was sentenced to five years' penal servitude.

If an ad – any ad – is to fulfil its purpose, it has to contain an element of deception. In this respect, all Lonely Hearts ads constitute identity fraud to an extent. Yet the sort of identity fraud perpetrated in the 1890s was considerably more malevolent than that of fifty years beforehand. Schoolboys who dressed in women's clothes for the sake of playing a practical joke on some poor unsuspecting gentleman were now replaced by swindles of a far more criminal nature. Furthermore, these swindles were now almost always aimed at women.

Take Evans Wood, alias Sir Henry Onequi, alias Baron Musgrave. Wood ran a palmistry business in New York, where he promoted himself as 'Palmist to the Queen'. Following a string of scams and having deserted not just one wife but two, he ended up in London, a metropolis so enormous and anonymous that it enabled Wood to reinvent himself yet again. In 1899, he placed the following ad in a matrimonial newspaper:

> Matrimony. Wanted, by an American gentleman, a wife who will be willing to make America her home. He has independent means, beautiful home; looks and figure most desired. Travels four months out of the year. Mosgrave, 295, Strand. W.C.

The ad was answered by a twenty-two-year-old barmaid living in Catford named Gladys Fenton – 'for fun,' she told the court. Wood asked if he could come and see her that Saturday night at eight o'clock; time was short, he claimed, since he hoped for a speedy marriage so that they could set off for Paris together. He arrived at her house and immediately asked her to marry him, whilst literally still standing on the doorstep. Miss Fenton accepted. When she was quizzed about this episode in court by Mr D'Eyncourt, the prosecutor, it caused quite some merriment.

> Mr D'Eyncourt: Straight off? (Laughter).
> Miss Fenton: Yes.
> Mr D'Eyncourt: No preliminary observations?
> Miss Fenton: No. (Laughter).

The following day, Miss Fenton was delighted to receive a lengthy love letter from her new amour. It began:

> I have heard of being struck by the great love passion (? poison) called love, but thought it was a very absurd thing. But I guess

I have got the disease at last. Will describe my symptoms: very nervous; restless nights; smoke like a furnace; actually lost appetite for breakfast; keep thinking of a face I have met at No. 107, and those eyes . . .

About ten days later, Wood arrived at Miss Fenton's house accompanied by a man he introduced as Judge Gilmore. Gilmore read out what sounded like a marriage ceremony, had the couple sign some papers and pronounced them husband and wife.

Wood then proceeded to borrow some money from Miss Fenton, telling her he was expecting some funds to be transferred to him from America any day. Predictably, she then never saw him again – until they met in court, that is, where she testified that he had 'seemed so genuine that she thought he was all right'. Wood received the exceptionally harsh sentence of five years in prison, ostensibly just for the theft of some money, three gold rings, an umbrella and a quilt. What he was really being punished for, it would seem, was his involvement in Lonely Hearts ads.

As usual, however, society's harshest moral censure fell on the female victims of these scams. Women like Gladys Knowles, Hannah Tring, Emma Grimwood, Mary-Ann Dormer and Gladys Fenton were widely considered to have demonstrated 'amazing stupidity and credulity', as one judge put it. It was their own fault, was the implication; they were asking for it. 'Of course no girl with nice feelings would ever answer a matrimonial advertisement. Still there are some silly, giddy, young things who might be tempted to do so out of pure love of fun or to see what would happen. Many a girl has had bitter cause to remember her folly.' This article in *Reynolds's* in 1898 went on to advise young women to 'have nothing to say to the artfully specious advertiser whose cleverly designed "need of a wife" is only a net to catch silly forward girls to their own misery'.

Adjoining the article in *Reynolds's* was an enormous ad for Hudson's Soap. 'Shirts, cuffs, and collars washed with Hudson's Soap are thoroughly washed, therefore remain much longer clean – with about half the usual labour,' ran the strapline. It was an attempt to appeal to the unconscious desires of married women that, in many ways, mirrored the way Lonely Hearts ads were designed to appeal to the unconscious desires of single women. Con-men in particular had to be experts in female psychology. In all honesty, who, finding themselves in the desperate position that many nineteenth-century working- and middle-class women did, would find it easy to turn down an offer of marriage from the likes of Charles Leman, a 'Civil servant, tall, fair, thirty; pay £150, Churchman, literary, energetic'? It ticked almost all the boxes. Or from someone as well-settled and keen to commit as Frederick Hall, 'Mechanic (32) . . . view early marriage'? Evans Wood, 'an American gentleman' with 'independent means, beautiful home', who liked to travel a lot, was a similarly attractive-sounding proposition. After all, advertising of any kind is, at its core, a form of seduction.

Chapter Nine

A True Comrade and Friend

KATH BOOTHMAN'S FAMILY is a rare one. In her house, the fact that her grandparents met through a Lonely Hearts ad is not a secret. Conversely, it is a piece of family history that has been passed down through the generations with pride, and rightly so — it is a tale of love and duty, of missed opportunities and snatched second chances. More than anything, it is a tale of romance.

Kath's grandmother, Gertrude Judd — or Gertie, as she was known — was born in 1870 in Dover Castle in Kent, where her father Alfred Judd, an army chaplain, was stationed. Seventeen years later her mother died of a chest infection on the morning of Christmas Day, with the result that Gertie, as the eldest of seven sisters, suddenly found herself thrust into the role of chief home-maker. By 1891 the Judds had moved to Portsmouth, and Gertie had got a job as a teacher in an elementary school.

Opportunities to meet men remained extremely limited, however, and in 1895 Gertie spotted the following ad in the paper: 'Young man, 28 years of age, would like to meet a young lady with a view to matrimony.' The ad had been placed by one John Burnicle. Born in Sunderland in 1866 to a property developer and his wife, Jack (which is what everyone called him) was by this time living in Rickmansworth and, like Gertie, was working as a teacher. The two exchanged letters, and within weeks they met in person and he asked her to marry him.

But Gertie faced the same dilemma as many of her sex. Although teachers constituted the largest category of professional women in this period, for most it was not a career that was compatible with marriage. And, although she liked Jack very much, she was not yet ready to sacrifice the new-found freedom that her career gave her. After years of drudgery, cooking and cleaning for her father and sisters, the prospect of having another family to take care of probably did not appeal.

So, after much thought, Gertie turned Jack down, and they lost touch.

The years passed. Gertie spent some time at Lincoln Training College studying for her teacher's certificate, but by 1902 had returned to Portsmouth and was back at work, now fully qualified. She was thirty-two and, by the standards of the day, an old maid. But then, while going through a pile of old papers, her younger sister Miriam happened across a letter of Jack's. Thinking that Gertie must have had quite a soft spot for him to have bothered to keep hold of their correspondence all these years, Miriam wrote to the address at the top of the letter to find out what had become of him. She received a reply from Jack's sister to the effect that he had got married, but his wife had died of tuberculosis and he had moved back home. He was in very low spirits, she added. And so, without passing on the information she had received from Jack's sister, Miriam asked Gertie over a cup of tea one day if she had ever regretted giving Jack up. Gertie admitted that she had, but that there was no point in dwelling on it because he was sure to be married by now. Miriam said no more, but wrote to Jack's sister again suggesting that, if he were to write to Gertie, the letter was likely to be very well received.

Jack jumped at the chance, and the friendship was quickly renewed. He and Gertie met up that summer in Tynemouth, where Gertie was on holiday with some friends, then continued to write to each other for another year until Jack proposed – again. This time Gertie did not hesitate to accept him. She still kept him waiting a while, though (perhaps she wanted more time to reap the rewards of being a qualified teacher, with its improved status and salary), and it was not until 6 April 1906 that they were married in Portsmouth.

Gertie and Jack

Gertie immediately gave up her career, as expected, and they moved to Jack's home town of Sunderland, where he took up a position as headmaster of Hilton Road School. It proved to be a long and happy marriage, albeit one tinged by sadness. A year in, Gertie gave birth to a stillborn baby, followed a couple of years by a little boy who was to die of meningitis at the age of two. However, in 1912 — by which time Gertie was forty-two, and had pretty much given up hope of ever having more children — they adopted the two-year-old daughter of Jack's first wife's widowed sister. Then, to everyone's surprise and delight, the first year of the First World War brought them a daughter of their own, who they named Kathleen. The four of them lived happily together until 1927, when Jack sadly died of pneumonia at the age of sixty.

The most surprising aspect of Jack and Gertie's life story is not that they met through a Lonely Hearts ad, but rather that they told their family about it. (It was their granddaughter, Kath Boothman, who then kindly told me about it, in response to an ad that I placed in a local paper.) One searches and searches for similar couples, but to no avail. The evidence simply is not there. Advertising for love was a taboo subject, and not one that people were willing to admit to – not even to their children. Hence the historian comes up against a considerable wall of silence on the subject. When asked, most of those who lived through the first half of the twentieth century will confidently (albeit misguidedly) assert that Lonely Hearts ads did not exist in their day. But the fact is that they did, increasingly so, and in a form that was gradually evolving in response to the great upheavals that British society experienced during this period.

Gertie was not the only woman of her generation to postpone marriage for the sake of her career. By 1911 teachers like her numbered 180,000, while other professions that were increasingly open to women without independent means included becoming a governess, a nurse or a clerical worker. Higher education was also an option. Developments such as trousers and the bicycle further enabled women to escape the fast-fading strictures of the Victorian moral code. The prospect of political emancipation presented itself with the foundation of the Women's Social and Political Union (WSPU) in 1903, while sexual liberation also became a point of discussion, in part due to the emergence of Freudian theory. The British essayist and physician Havelock Ellis declared that sex was one of 'the great driving forces of human life', and popular culture, in particular the cinema, reflected this new openness. 'No wonder girls of the older days, before movies, were so modest and bashful. They never saw Clara Bow and William Haines ... If we did not see such examples ... where would we get the idea of being "hot"?' commented one seventeen-year-old.

'In these progressive times, when woman is entering in new chan-

nels of employment, of public work, and of private enterprise . . .
an opportunity to correspond with the other sex is an education in
itself.' So believed the crusading humanitarian journalist W.T. Stead
who, in 1898, founded *Round-About* magazine, which pioneered an
entirely new sort of Lonely Hearts ad: the 'companionship' ad.

Those who subscribed to *Round-About* did so on the understanding that 'they commit themselves to nothing except a desire
to make the acquaintance of some of the opposite sex with a view
to a Circular correspondence . . . it should never be assumed as a
matter of course that the correspondence must have a matrimonial issue'. In other words, the proclaimed purpose of the magazine
was to help people find a companion, rather than necessarily a
spouse. Thus respectable women were for the first time presented
with an opportunity to explore their sexuality in a way that involved
neither marriage nor prostitution. It also offered the option of
men and women simply being friends, which was a radical new
concept promoted in the pre-war period by a number of progressive thinkers, including H.G. Wells, Dora Russell and Marie Stopes.
It revealed the emergence in the late Victorian and early Edwardian
period of a new sort of young middle-class woman for whom the
dull vagaries of settling down to a respectable, domestic, married
existence was not the be-all and end-all. There was too much fun
to be had first; and, with new forms of birth control such as the
contraceptive cap increasingly becoming available, the risks also
diminished.

And, indeed, a good number of those who advertised in *Round-
About* specified that they 'require friendship, not marriage' or 'want
correspondence for exchange of ideas'. The women featured tended
to be the enlightened kind: they included school teachers, private
nurses and the daughters of solicitors, clergymen and tradesmen. A
twenty-two-year-old journalist from Middlesex – 'considered by
some to be handsome, by others to be merely passable' – described
herself as 'rather a Bohemian; has been brought up with boys, and

B. 129. MIDDLESEX.—33; tall; slight; rather fair; grey eyes; healthy, domesticated; cyclist; fairly educated and of refined tastes; but not accomplished; affectionate disposition; fond of reading, and deeply interested in the religious questions of the age; broad views; Unitarian tendencies; I should like to correspond with a gentleman not older than 45, nor younger than 34; cyclist; tall and strong; rather dark; interested in similar subjects; an honourable, even-tempered, sympathetic man; one preferably who, like Tennyson's hero in "In Memoriam," has "fought his doubts and gathered strength;" a true comrade and friend.

B. 132. LANCASHIRE.—36; rather fair; of medium size; fond of literature, travelling, and cycling; musical; trained nurse, and experienced housekeeper; daughter of English minister in good position; small means later on; wishes to correspond with broad-minded man of refined and similar tastes, active and healthy, with a view to friendship or marriage.

B. 133. YORKSHIRE.—Tradesman's daughter; age 31; Churchwoman; fair; dark hair; slight; refined; of average ability; domesticated; fond of children and animals; desires correspondence with a temperate and honourable gentleman of fair position; age 32—43.

B. 134. DERBYSHIRE.—Lady; medium height; fair; blue eyes; aged 35, but looks younger; good-tempered, cheerful; thoroughly domesticated; well educated; fond of music and reading; being far from few surviving relatives, and meeting only with friends of my own sex, would like to correspond, on any interesting subject, with refined and cultivated man about same age.

B. 135. MIDDLESEX.—Age 33; medium height; slight; dark hair; dark grey eyes; considered good-looking by friends; good taste; refined; sociable; good manager and housekeeper; domesticated; well educated; said to have tact; healthy; cheerful; affectionate; enjoy recreations; father a professional gentleman, but has been dead for 10 years; have had to work hard as teacher to help mother and younger brothers; necessity over now; well connected; wishes to correspond with a high principled, earnest, reasonably ambitious man of strong character; one who has had difficulties to overcome preferred; broad-minded and educated; age not less than 36; one who does not think a woman has lost her *womanliness* and love of home because circumstances force her to be independent.

B. 136. DERBYSHIRE.—Age 27; orphan; tall; travelled; good connections: Church of England; fond of home and outdoor pursuits; fluent German; sing pretty well; pleasant appearance; educated; small private income; desires to correspond with good sensible man, between 27 and 40; Church of England; one I could look up to and respect.

B. 137. YORKSHIRE.—Age 24; tall and slight; well educated, musical, and domesticated; retiring, studious disposition; very fond of reading; has a dreary life in a quiet provincial town, where there is no opportunity of making any congenial friendship; prefers someone with similar tastes, literary or artistic, who would like a correspondence for exchange of ideas and friendship; circumstances immaterial; congenial and sympathetic comrade desired.

B. 138. MIDDLESEX.—Brunette; not tall; of French origin; good family; educated in London and Paris; accustomed to good society; intellectual and varied tastes; would like to correspond with a gentleman in French or English; in a good position; of an honourable character; and possessing broad views; and who is seeking a partner for life; age from 40 to 60.

A page of ads from women in *Round-About* magazine, 15 July 1898 looks at life from rather a masculine point of view, but is not a "woman's rights girl'". She sought 'a man friend, not a future husband, as she does not wish to marry for at least six years . . . birth immaterial; no spiritualists or theosophists'.

Those women who did seek marriage generally demanded it be of the progressive kind. One dreamed of meeting someone 'whose ideal of marriage is, like her own, that of the Brownings, and of John Stuart Mill', another someone 'who, like Tennyson's hero in *In Memoriam*, has "fought his doubts and gathered strength"; a true comrade and friend'. Such literary references abound, for *Round-About*'s clientele tended to be of a highly educated sort. And some of them clearly had great success. As one satisfied customer told it:

> I was in bed resting after a hard day's work house-moving. The May Circular had come the evening before, and to amuse myself I began looking . . . I saw A——, liked the [ad], jumped up, dressed, and wrote my letter. Since then I have had a small library of letters, and have written the same. We spent three days together in each other's company. I was accountable to no-one, nor was he, and we found out more of each other than we could have done during a year of ordinary wooing.

Three weeks later, they were engaged to be married.

There were many, however, who strongly disapproved of the kind of relationship that emerged out of a courtship period of just three weeks. A string of lurid court cases in the opening decade of the new century confirmed concerns that the freedoms now available to women could, and would, lead to their moral downfall. In 1901, four months after Edward VII's coronation, readers of *The Times* gleefully devoured details of the trial of Frank and Edith Jackson, co-conspirators in a plot to use Lonely Hearts ads to lure young women into their cult, then force them into sex.

'Gentleman, 30, handsome, independent, refined, highly educated, exemplary habits, desires matrimony,' ran one ad that the Jacksons placed in a weekly newspaper. The result was a flood of letters, mostly from young women living in the suburbs. Frank Jackson, under the alias Theodore Horos, would then invite them to his house in Regent's Park, introduce them to Edith, whom he pretended was his mother (she was twelve years older than him) and propose marriage, on the understanding that they immediately move in with him and surrender all their possessions. He also revealed himself to be the founder and head of a religious order known as the Theocratic Unity. The cult's watchwords were poverty, chastity and obedience, and members were expected to follow a strictly fruitarian diet. As part of the elaborate initiation ceremony, Frank had sex with the women against their will while Edith held them down. Following one such incident involving sixteen-year-old Daisy Adams, the court was told that Frank said to Edith, 'Welcome our little daughter. She is one of us.'

One has to sympathise with the plight of the likes of Daisy Adams. Naïve as she was to move in with a man she had only just met, it was her desperation to get married that led her to reply to the Jacksons' ad in the first place. Women of the sort who advertised in *Round-About* solely for a companion remained in the minority. For most, marriage was still the goal.

> I think we would all prefer
> Marriage with strife
> Than to be left on the shelf
> And be nobody's wife.

ran a popular music-hall song. The trend towards marriage in its most traditional form, which had begun in the Victorian era, continued. Despite the slight increase in the number of professions open to middle-class women, employment possibilities for working-class women remained highly restricted. More were finding work as secretaries and in shops, but fewer as live-in servants and in the textile industry. A little less than 30 per cent of the female population earned any wage at all. With so few jobs available, and most so badly paid, the majority of single women still had to rely on a male relation for financial support. '[E]ssentially a trade on the part of woman – the exchange of her person for the means of subsistence' was how the suffragist Cicely Hamilton described marriage in 1909. Yet to attain this, one was expected to submit to society's deeply hypocritical double standards: '. . . She has been brought up in the belief that her profession is marriage and motherhood; yet though poverty may be pressing on her – though she may be faced with actual lack of the necessities of life – she must not openly express her desire to enter that profession, and earn her bread in the only way for which she is fitted. She must stand aside and wait – indefinitely . . .'

Some, however, refused to 'stand aside and wait', and so it was

Sales assistants outside a dress shop in the early twentieth century

that matrimonial newspapers continued to flourish. In 1904 the *Matrimonial Times* appeared in its third incarnation, this time with many of its ads styled in the third person, a throwback to John Houghton's *modus operandi*. Its early editions included a suspicious preponderance of startlingly attractive women and impossibly eligible men, with some of the ads appearing repeatedly for months on end. It was presumably an attempt to increase business, and if so it worked, for the *Matrimonial Times* was to run for the next sixty-seven years.

In 1909 it was joined on the news-stands by the Sheffield-based *International Matrimonial Gazette*, later the *Matrimonial Gazette*. This began as a mere ten-page pamphlet, but by 1913 it was much longer and more expensively produced, and featured ads that would have been inconceivable fifty years earlier – for example, the one from a twenty-seven-year-old gentleman, 'belonging to one of the highest Parsee families in India, father holding one of the highest positions in that country, well known in the best English society'. Originally from Bombay, he was now living in Yorkshire and studying architecture. Men were by no means exempt from the tyranny of what society considered to be 'normal', and those who remained celibate risked the stigma of being accused of being gay, particularly in the aftermath of the Oscar Wilde trial.

The establishment of the *Matrimonial Mascot* (1910), the *Matrimonial Standard* (1914) and the *Matrimonial Circle* (1914) demonstrates a continuing demand for the service that these newspapers provided, for women in particular – of whom, the census of 1911 revealed, there was a 'surplus' of 1.3 million, in large part due to a recent mass exodus of men to the colonies. For some, however, their involvement with Lonely Hearts ads was not merely a practical response to a problem, but rather a quest to inject a little romance into their life. Women were widely encouraged to be 'in love' from an early age, and novels like Ethel M. Dell's *The Way of an Eagle* (1912), which was reprinted twenty-seven times in its first three years alone, gave hope to those still in search of their knight in shining armour. It was also becoming less and less acceptable to admit to marrying for material reasons, rather than for love, with the result that middle-class expectations of marriage soared. Quite simply, people wanted more.

The outbreak of the First World War led to the emergence of an entirely new sort of Lonely Hearts ad: the Lonely Soldier ad. These first appeared in *T.P.'s Weekly*, a literary magazine founded by the Irish journalist and politician T.P. O'Connor. The 12 February 1916 edition, for example, featured an ad from a 'Lonely Young Officer, up to his neck in Flanders' who 'would like to correspond with young lady (age 18–20), cheery and good looking'. These sorts of ads soon managed to inveigle themselves into the mainstream press as well, in particular the *Daily Mail*.

Yet at the same time as millions of young men were 'up to [their] neck in Flanders', others behaved as if nothing had changed, continuing to cheat, lie and steal their way through life. On 30 June 1915, Gerald Fitzgerald sailed into Liverpool from New York. He settled first in London and then in Manchester, where he immediately placed an ad in a local newspaper: 'Bachelor (35), good income and appearances, wishes to meet refined lady, preferably with a small income or capital. Genuine references.' He received 179 replies to this and two further ads, many of which he responded to, promising marriage at the same time as asking to borrow some money to enable him to take out a patent for the automatic lubrication of motor engines. In this way he managed to extort a total of £3,455 from various women in the course of just one year, partly because, the court was told at his trial, he was such 'an agreeable companion, who possessed in a remarkable degree the power of exciting the curiosity of women'. Fitzgerald was sentenced to eight years' penal servitude for theft and bigamy.

It was not just men who were guilty of such behaviour. In the case of Hannah Donaldson, heard at Bradford Court in 1917, it was revealed that at least one of the men she met via an ad had been persuaded to give her so much money that in the end he went bank-rupt. '[H]ow many fools there [are] in the world,' marvelled the judge. In a way, though, it was a victory for equal opportunities, as women began to exploit men in the very same way that they them-selves had for centuries been exploited.

For many, however, all the war offered was loss. The writer and pacifist Vera Brittain recalled a 'startling' ad that she saw in a news-paper in 1915: 'Lady, fiancé killed, will gladly marry officer totally blinded or otherwise incapacitated by the War.' In a letter to her own fiancé, Brittain speculated that the advertiser '. . . does not want to face the dreariness of an unoccupied and unattached old-maidenhood. But the only person she loved is dead; all men are alike to her and it is a matter of indifference whom she marries, so she thinks she may as well marry someone who really needs her.' She 'will perhaps find relief for her sorrow in devoting her life to him'. Brittain then wondered whether 'anyone will answer it? It is purely a business arrangement, with an element of self-sacrifice which redeems it from utter sordidness. Quite an idea, isn't it?'

Quite an idea it was, and similarly heartbreaking ads continued to appear in newspapers and magazines both during and after the war, a testament to the number of lives that had been destroyed by the fighting. For instance, a 1926 edition of *The Matchmaker*, a matri-monial newspaper founded that same year, features an ad from a nurse named Theresa in Bristol who explains how: 'In 1914 I was engaged to a soldier and when he was killed thought I should never want anyone else, not have I until lately'; as well as one from a 'young widowed lady (Scotch), newly arrived in London, seeks matri-mony for the third time, having lost first husband in the war and second husband in aeroplane accident . . .' This is a vivid account of a life blighted by grief, summed up in a single sentence.

Women like Theresa faced a difficult world, post-war. With three-quarters of a million men killed in combat, there was a severe shortage of potential husbands, which was exacerbated by the

Spanish-flu epidemic of 1918. In the new *palais de danse* halls it was common to see two women dancing together; 'the mateless multitude,' the *Daily Mail* called them. By 1921 Britain had a 'surplus' of 1.7 million women, with the result that many of those who had always assumed they would marry were forced to accept that they might not. Others, however, refused to be thwarted, and, for the first time, the number of Lonely Hearts ads placed by women exceeded those placed by men.

And so the Lonely Hearts industry continued to flourish, buoyed in part by the occasional success story. It was an ad in a Bavarian newspaper in 1920 that brought Pope Benedict XVI's parents together, while, closer to home, Charlie Clarkson and Beatrice Pimm found love the same way. The couple originally met in 1916 when Beatrice was living in a private hotel on London's Brompton Square

One possible solution to the shortage of male dance partners (*Punch*, 1923)

that Charlie had happened to visit. They corresponded for three years and, in 1919 when he was demobbed, he proposed. She turned him down, however, claiming that she was already engaged.

Four years later, having still not found himself a suitable wife, Charlie contacted a marriage journal, which sent him a list of names. Among them was a Miss B. Pimm. By this time Beatrice was thirty and still living at home in Witney, Oxfordshire, with her father (a butcher), mother and five siblings. Charlie wrote to her at once and they arranged to meet. 'When I knocked on the door,' he recalled:

> her mother opened it. I told her I was Mr Clarkson, from London, and asked if her daughter had got a letter that morning? She said 'No', but her daughter was expecting one, and called to Beatrice. When Beatrice opened the door we recognised each other immediately. She said, 'Good God, it's Charlie!' and I said, 'Damn it, it's Beatrice.'

He invited her out for a walk, and by the time they returned they were engaged. They got married in the early summer of 1923.

Women like Beatrice, desperate to escape their suburban, lower-middle-class existence, were brought to life in a radio play, entitled *Matrimonial News*, by Tyrone Guthrie, broadcast on the BBC in 1928. It is midday, and thirty-two-year-old Florence Kippings is sitting in a cheap restaurant on the Strand, drinking a cup of coffee. Her father died when she was twelve, so now she lives alone with her mother in Bromley above the sewing shop that they run together.

Today, however, Florence has taken the day off work in order to meet a man – 'Bachelor age 38, 5 foot 8 inches, fresh complexion, dark hair, blue eyes, own business in the North' – whose ad she spotted in the *Matrimonial News*. 'Such a paper as *Matrimonial News* really does exist,' notes Guthrie in the stage directions. 'It is obtainable at many book-stalls, and is not in the least indecent.'

Modernist in style, this is a daring, expressionistic play, far ahead of its time. Guthrie instructed that 'many of the lines are to be regarded more as rhythm and jingle than as "sense" ... By this means, it is hoped to convey the half-formed ideas and images surging, tumbling, churning in the consciousness of Miss Kippings ...' Thus Florence explains that she has 'come here to get away – to escape'. She is 'so tired – *so* tired' of being at home:

> I was so lonely –
> There's no-one at home –
> I mean mother and me ...

She tries to imagine what other people are saying about her:

> She's getting on –
> Getting nippy –
> Getting old-maidish –
> It's the neck that gives them away ...

There is a further problem, too: 'I don't know any men ... well, there's Mr Mildmay – he's the gentleman from next door – it's a tobacco business and newsagency – he's over seventy ...'

And so Florence answers a Lonely Hearts ad. Sipping her coffee, she daydreams about what her prospective husband might say to her when he eventually arrives:

> I've been waiting for you –
> I knew that somewhere I would find you –
> That somewhere you were hiding –
> I want to take care of you –
> To protect you –
> Little girl –
> I love you – I love you – I love you ...

In the background is the sound of an orchestra playing a swooning waltz. It is intentionally filmic in feel; indeed, Florence mentions that she goes to the cinema at least once a week. Greta Garbo is her favourite actress.

As the play reaches a climax, her thoughts take a darker turn. 'Come on – come on Greta – take my hand . . .' implores her imaginary date, 'cruelly, coaxing,' according to the stage directions. The implication is that Florence is living in a fantasy world where she thinks she is at the centre of a great romance of the type she has seen so many times on the big screen. Real life quickly intrudes, however: her courage fails her, she panics and leaves, only to get back on the train and return to her depressing existence living in Bromley with her mother.

At least, though, she had money of her own to pay for the train fare, as well as for writing paper, a stamp and a cup of coffee while she waited for her date to arrive. '[Mother] doesn't know I'm here – how could she find out – I'm just going up to town mother – Alice's going too – we're going to Ponting's sale . . . white sale – white lie – well? My own money – why shouldn't I?'

Florence was just one of millions of women who experienced new economic freedoms in the post-war period. Manpower shortages had released women into the heady world of traditionally male professions, and so it was that a newspaper investigation into the Lonely Hearts industry in 1921 found that most of the women who advertised were in white-collar employment – working as secretaries, clerks, teachers.

The First World War had also expanded women's social horizons. Many were no longer willing to submit to the Victorian-era demand that unmarried, lower- and lower-middle-class young women ought to remain at home beside the fireside, pretending to be fascinated by needlework. And so they became regular features not only, shockingly, of pubs, but of churches, cinemas and the local promenade, which, with the decline of the music halls so popular in Edwardian

Britain, had become the primary venues for meeting members of the opposite sex. According to the *Daily Mirror* in 1919, a typical post-war woman was frivolous, insincere and 'spoiled by war-time pleasures'. The most progressive ('flappers') even asserted their right to get drunk, smoke cigarettes, wear lipstick and cut their hair short. 'The war has produced a new type of girl,' noted the activist historian Louise Creighton, 'absolutely independent, very often wild and undisciplined [who] . . . laughs and screams in the streets [and] is eager for any fun and nonsense'.

And for many, that's indeed what Lonely Hearts ads were – a bit of 'fun and nonsense'. The 'companionship' ad of the sort pioneered by *Round-About* became increasingly popular, with a number appearing in the *Daily Express* in the 1920s, among other places, that did not even allude to marriage. Rather, it was an opportunity for

Trying to catch a husband (*Strand Magazine*, 1923)

these newly empowered young women to explore their sexuality without having to submit to the shackles of marriage. In a telling shift in semantics, many describe themselves as a 'bachelor girl' rather than a 'spinster', while the term 'sporty' also emerged as advertising shorthand for someone who was urban, modern and open-minded.

One of the most popular forums for 'companionship' ads was *The Link* magazine. Established in 1915, it was, according to the editor, 'intended to help those in need of friends. Its primary purpose is not matrimony . . .' And yet the entire magazine consists of ads from ladies wanting to meet gentlemen, and vice versa. Most are written in a brief, straightforward manner, but a few do veer towards the risqué: 'Lothario, London West, 30, ex officer, wants cuddlesome girls, fond of rivers, dancing, pleasure'; 'Widow, (London W), greatly interested in discipline, would like to hear from others, both sexes'. It was later discovered that this last one had been placed by a woman who had twice been convicted for brothel-keeping.

Ads like these did nothing to improve the reputation of Lonely

A Cinema designed for both Lovers and Picture-Lovers (*The Humorist*, 1925)

Hearts ads, which was already taking a battering as a result of the trial in France of Henri Désiré Landru, also known as 'the French Bluebeard', who in 1921 was found guilty of murdering ten women he had met via a newspaper. This led *The Times*, among others, to reassert the fact that it did not accept Lonely Hearts ads of any kind for publication.

It is no surprise, therefore, that the authorities soon began to focus on the personal columns of the popular press. In 1921 *The Link*'s publisher, Alfred Barrett, was charged with conspiring to corrupt public morals, not only 'by introducing men to women for fornication', but also 'by introducing men to men for unnatural and grossly indecent practices'. The authorities were first alerted to *The Link* by the chance arrest for fraud of fifty-seven-year-old Walter Birks from Carlisle, upon whose person were found a number of love letters from William Smyth, a twenty-year-old Belfast clerk, whom he had met through an ad in *The Link*. The letters were described by the judge in Barrett's trial as 'the most filthy he had ever heard read'. On further investigation of the magazine, ads like the one from an 'Oxonian . . . 26' who sought someone 'brilliant, courteous, humorous, poet, future novelist, in love with beauty despite cosmic insignificance, masculine . . .' led prosecutors to conclude that it was indeed a hotbed of homosexual intrigue. They told the court that it 'contained hundreds of advertisements from men who described themselves as "artistic and musical"'. 'Unconventional' also functioned as a codeword for gay, though some did not even bother with euphemisms: 'Reggie (London SE), young bachelor, lonely, affectionate, sincere, musical, theatrical, wishes to meet nice looking young male about 20, if possible share rooms, also week ends. Photo appreciated.'

The fact, however, that 'theatrical' 'Reggie' felt able to advertise so openly his wish to 'share rooms' with a 'nice looking young male' is evidence that attitudes towards homosexuality were slowly changing. It is highly likely that personal ads had been used as a way for those outside the mainstream to make contact with each other for many decades, possibly ever since the seventeenth century when they first emerged, but this is impossible to prove. With homosexuality illegal, ads had by their very nature to be discreetly phrased. This is why *The Link* trial caused such a sensation, revealing as it did for the first time a hidden world of homosexual courtship.

In the end, poor Barrett was sentenced to two years' hard labour and *The Link* was forced to close. The trial had effectively been a battleground to police post-war sexual morality. It was not the only one. In 1928, Thomas Owen, editor of *The Matchmaker*, sued *John Bull* magazine for libel in response to three derogatory articles published there the year before, entitled 'Will Anybody Marry Me?', 'Amazing Marriage Mart' and 'Infamous Editor Exposed'. Owen told the court that, as a result of the articles, he had 'been held up to ridicule, odium, hatred and contempt, and that the business of *The Matchmaker* . . . has been injured'.

It is indisputable that the sort of ads that were appearing in *The Matchmaker* by this date demonstrate a significant shift in intention, particularly among men. A sixty-year-old 'Lonely Gentleman' who has been separated from his wife for twenty-five years seeks a 'partnership (marriage when possible)'; others seek 'companionship', with no mention of marriage; others are even more open in their search for sexual thrills, for example the 'Business man (married), with money to spend on frolics &c., living in nearby small town, [who] visits London almost daily, age 40, well built, tall and important looking, genteel, considered debonair, generous and kind,' who stipulates that he 'wishes to meet lady, married or single, who can instruct in all the very latest dances including Charlestown and Tango; must be someone with own private floor space'.

It was revealed in court that a journalist for *John Bull* by the name of Moseley had approached *The Matchmaker* posing as a married man, and had still received a list of the women it had on its books. 'I thought that he was entitled to something for his money, so I decided to send him a few platonic introductions,' protested Owen when questioned about this. Moseley had also secured an interview with a Miss X, who was one of the women he had been offered. He told the court:

> She said that she had been sent two men, whom she described as 'rotters', and that one was a half-caste man from Mexico. She said: 'As soon as I saw him I bolted'. Of the other, she said that he was old enough to be her grandfather; that he was fat, and smelt of drink; and that he certainly did not want to get married.

Moseley then commented that, 'She was pathetically eager to get "fixed up", as she put it', thereby demonstrating his immense hypocrisy by criticising an unmarried woman for looking for someone to marry, even though from the day she was born it would have been drummed into her that, in the words of E.M. Delafield in *Thank Heaven Fasting* (1932): '... a woman's failure or success in life depended entirely upon whether or not she succeeded in getting a husband. It was not, even, a question of marrying well, although mothers with pretty and attractive daughters naturally hoped for that. But any husband at all was better than none.' Moseley clearly felt that he had the moral majority on his side, pompously telling the court that the aim of his articles was 'to expose an evil'.

Yet it was an 'evil' that was all but impossible to police consistently. Lonely Hearts ads have always existed outside the realm of family supervision, and this, compounded by the anonymity they offer, lays them open to the suspicion that they act as secretive guides to all kinds of immorality. In 1928, one investigative journalist alleged that 15,000 women a year were disappearing into the white slave trade, many as a result of answering a Lonely Hearts ad. It was an enormously exaggerated claim, but one that pandered cleverly to those who were convinced that such ads represented a gateway into unimaginable dangers – sexual and otherwise. In reality, these were merely an expression of a range of moral and social anxieties that were bubbling up as a result of the growth of cities, women's increasing independence, the collapse of a number of long-standing rules of courtship (for example, the need for a woman to be accompanied by a chaperone at all times), and so on – anxieties that were only to intensify throughout the 1930s as a spate of court cases further confirmed the tempting opportunities Lonely Hearts ads offered to frauds, bigamists and thieves.

This was not the only reason why there was a slight decrease in the number of Lonely Hearts ads placed during the 1930s, particularly from women. With the return of a huge number of men from the colonies, as well as a flood of political refugees from Europe, the gender imbalance began to right itself – with the result that a woman's chances of finding someone to marry without turning to the newspapers for help improved somewhat. Among fifteen- to forty-nine-year-olds, the proportion of women to men fell from 110 per cent in 1931 to 106 per cent in 1939, while the marriage rate per 1,000 single women over fifteen rose from 57.3 in 1931–5 to 73.3 in 1936–40; it also rose for single men over fifteen, from 62.6 to 78.7. Among the middle classes, it remained usual to meet one's future husband or wife through family, church or work connections. The working classes tended to court one another in cinemas and dance palaces, at Sunday School or cycling club, or on an evening walk.

But then came the Second World War.

Its outbreak did not immediately prevent the publication of the big-hitting matrimonial newspapers – namely the *Matrimonial Times, Post* and *Gazette*, which since 1919 had claimed to have the largest circulation of any of them – and for good reason. Writing in 1940, George Orwell remarked that 'Papers like the *Exchange and Mart*, for instance, or *Cage-Birds*, or the *Oracle*, or *Prediction*, or the *Matrimonial Times*, only exist because there is a definite demand for them, and they reflect the minds of their readers as a great national daily with a circulation of millions cannot possibly do.' Assuming Orwell was right, a browse through these newspapers suggests a strong desire to forget that the war was happening, reading as they do like a parallel universe in which it goes almost unmentioned. Instead, what is notable is the number of advertisers living abroad: a single edition of the *Matrimonial Times* from 1944 features a bank clerk in Canada, an army lieutenant in India, a planter in Malaysia, a farmer in South Africa and a civil servant in the Sudan.

But the dedicated matrimonial newspapers were not able to stumble on for long. The only two to make it into the post-war era were the *Matrimonial Post* and the *Matrimonial Times*, the *Matrimonial Gazette* having folded in 1944 after more than thirty years of continuous publication. The January 1946 edition of the *Matrimonial Post* is dominated by ads from men attempting to adjust to life outside the military, among them a 'peace-time solicitor, at present R.A.F. Officer', a 'Diesel Engineer (civil occupation), now R.A.F. Sergt.' and a 'Wartime Castings Investigator, peace-time Chartered Accountant'. In addition, there is page after page of ads from widows in search of a new life. One of them – 'age 40, desperately lonely, tall, medium figure, C.E., fond of music, reading, gardening, ex Civil Servant, having furniture for six rooms, small Capital...' – is among the first to employ an abbreviation ('T.T.', meaning teetotal) of the sort that were later to become ubiquitous.

However, what is most striking about the ads featured in the decade or so following the war is their air of stifling conventionality. Modern readers are left in no doubt that the sexual revolution has yet to happen. Male advertisers seek a 'cheerful', 'affectionate', 'even-tempered' woman who is about five years younger than them and has a good figure. One twenty-seven-year-old bachelor just out of the RAF, 'wild oats sown', advertised in the *Matrimonial Post* in 1954 for a 'capable and forthright young lady age under 31 who wants a normal, full married life. She must be teetotal, not wear glasses, domestically capable . . .' Turning to the women, most seek a 'kind-hearted', 'home-loving', 'well-groomed' man who is about ten years older than them and has some income. Almost all reassure the prospective spouse that they are 'willing to give up work on marriage', while those who admit to being divorced clarify that they were the petitioner – in other words, they were not at fault. Some use everything they have got to try to make themselves sound like an appealing prospect: 'well-shaped hands' and 'good teeth' are among the boasts that are made.

Thus by the time Gertie Burnicle, née Judd, died in 1948 at the age of seventy-eight, most Lonely Hearts ads looked pretty similar to the one she had answered with such great good luck more than half a century earlier. However, there were exceptions. A husband or wife, a companion or friend, a sexual partner of the opposite sex or the same sex: the genre had evolved to encompass a far broader range of human desire than in centuries past. You just had to know where to look.

Chapter Ten

Electric Evenings

'WHAT IS THAT strange lump underneath the carpet?' wondered Sarah Burns as she sat down at her desk. It was 1972, and the first day of her new job running the small-ads department of *Private Eye*. Lifting up the carpet, she was dismayed to discover an enormous pile of unopened letters and cheques. It transpired that her predecessor in the job had been not only hopelessly disorganised, but also a bit of a drunk, and had hidden them there to avoid having to deal with all the missives from the lonely and/or amorous souls that fell through the *Eye*'s letterbox every day.

Mrs (later Lady) Burns, however, proved to be rather more methodical in the way she ran the department. She received far more ads than she had space to include, so one of her duties became assessing which were the more interesting ones; sometimes, she would even write back to the advertiser with an exhortation that they try a little harder with their composition.

But it was with the replies to the ads that Mrs Burns had the most fun. After assessing each envelope individually – the handwriting, the postmark, the brand of writing paper – it often became apparent that many of the respondents suffered from severely elevated aspirations, and might in fact be better suited to a different ad to the one to which they had replied. And so she would merrily 'mix up' the box numbers, redirecting each reply at her own discretion to whomever she felt would be the most suitable match! The result was that the magazine's Lonely Hearts section flourished under her watch.

When Mrs Burns first started at *Private Eye*, it was one of the few mainstream publications that carried Lonely Hearts ads, the visibility of which had declined dramatically over the course of the previous eighty years. Not only had they become exceptionally rare in the national and local newspapers, but in 1955 the *Matrimonial Post* had folded, seventy years after it was first founded. The *Matrimonial Times* stumbled on a little longer, attempting to drum up business by embarking on a PR blitz. In a 1961 interview for the London *Evening Star*, the *Matrimonial Times*'s editor, Eleanor Radford, offered her analysis of what men and women look for in a partner:

> Older women: they are interested in being comfortable; looks don't matter, but the man must be kind, generous and loving; they usually inquire about his bank balance. Older men: They always want someone younger than themselves – by at least 15 years – and the woman must primarily be affectionate and good-tempered. Young women: They specify no divorces, require details of height, build, education, income and looks of the man they would like to meet, and prefer one in a profession. Young men: All specify that the woman must be slim, and couple it with the words 'attractive', 'pretty' and 'good-looking'. And they prefer a girl with capital.

Mrs Radford also claimed that the number of people advertising in her newspaper had doubled in recent years.

In August 1961, however, the *Matrimonial Times* ceased publication once and for all, the last of its kind to fold. It was the end of an era. With dedicated matrimonial newspapers now no more, and the mainstream press still largely refusing to accept them, Lonely Hearts ads all but disappeared from the radar for a few years. Magazines like the *New Statesman* typically featured a plethora of classifieds from those looking for a holiday companion or somewhere to stay during the school holidays, but no Lonely Hearts ads; rather, they are indicative of how *little* progress society had made by this date. For instance: 'Impec. young woman expecting baby Aug. seeks accom. Will mind children, type, etc. Anything considered,' ran an ad in the *New Statesman* in 1960. Ask anyone who was young in the 1950s and '60s and they will almost certainly deny that Lonely Hearts ads even existed then. It was almost as if they had never been invented.

But why? The institution of marriage was more popular than ever: rates soared after the war, and by the 1950s more of Britain's men and women were getting married, and at a younger age, than at any other time in history. Yet, to some, it still seemed as difficult as ever to meet a prospective spouse. Among the working classes, the dance hall was 'the most popular place for meeting one's life partner: over a quarter of couples had met in this way', according to a 1959 Gallup poll. For the middle classes the opportunities were still rather more limited, as long as a number of long-standing restrictions on courtship remained in place The difficulties faced by educated, professional women in particular are conveyed in a short story that appeared in *Woman's Weekly* in 1960:

> . . . you were always expecting someone really exciting to be just around the corner. You went to each dance and social evening at the University hoping, and then you only met all the people you knew already. No tall, dark, handsome stranger flashed his cigarette case at you with a fascinating lift of the eyebrow.

The problem lay to some degree in women's inflated romantic expectations, acquired in part from the many pulp romance novels that sold in their millions. The reality was that, for the first time in a while, at least according to statistics, there were men to be had. Far

more had returned from the Second World War than from the First
World War, and by 1951 the gender imbalance had equalised among
those under thirty.

What is crucial to note, however, is just how profoundly private
the people of Britain were in the post-war period, and hence less
willing than ever to make their needs and desires public. For this
reason, the service provided by ads was largely replaced by agencies.
The most famous of these was the one run by Heather Jenner, who
in 1953 offered her own analysis of the need for them:

> There is so little home-entertaining, and no longer the big
> families with brothers and sisters and cousins to provide the
> nucleus of a wide social circle. Anyway, few can afford the
> activities which used to give opportunities for meeting and
> mating. 'I can't afford to go around much these days,' is the
> stock phrase of men and girls, old and young; and 'I have so
> little time to go out and find friends' is the equally well-used
> excuse of the doctor, lawyer, the business-woman, the welfare-
> worker or the girl who has to help at home . . . . 'They tell
> us to belong to clubs' one girl wrote to me. 'I hate clubs. I
> suppose I am definitely not clubbable. And when I go to cock-
> tail parties the hostess never gets around to introducing me to
> any single men.'

It is a story typical of the modern era.

Jenner, whose clients ranged 'from plumbers to peers and from
charladies to countesses', was quickly emulated by a number of
others who also saw a gap in the market. Correspondence clubs
were popular too, in particular niche ones like the Catholic
Introductions Bureau of the 1950s. The mainstream papers at first
refused to allow them to advertise – 'because of the bad name that
such bureaux had acquired on account of their seductive ads' – and
their ads were mainly seen in theatre programmes. This changed in

the 1960s; the Katherine Allen marriage bureau, for instance, advertised in the personal columns of the *Daily Telegraph* and the London *Evening Standard*, and others in the tabloids and the local press.

In 1965, a researcher for the Consumers' Association was sent to investigate the Katherine Allen marriage bureau. He found that those who signed up for membership could be divided roughly into two categories. There were the 'genuines' – that is, those who were widowed or divorced or who had recently returned from a stint abroad. Then there were the 'doubtfuls' – those looking solely for money or sex. He learned to be particularly suspicious of men over forty-five who had never been married at all, and later lobbied for the trade association to ban them entirely from their books. He also identified what he called the 'broken-wing' syndrome.

I found, as did most of the team, that there was a large proportion of lonely, introverted people out there who lacked what are now called interpersonal skills and in consequence felt unable to meet a member of the opposite sex without the use of an intermediary. The great problem there was that they were too keen to get tied into marriage and that presented other problems.

It is, in essence, an identical analysis to that offered by 'Y.M.' in his 1832 pamphlet on the subject.

Couples who did meet and marry with the help of an agency never admitted it, however. Jenner explained that:

Our married clients are careful never to tell their friends that they met through the Bureau. They concoct a story of a mutual friend who happened to introduce them, or an imaginary cocktail party or dance where they met, and, after years of repetition, actually come to believe it themselves. For this reason, although they recommend us to family and close friends, no one ever hears of the couple who have married through us, despite the fact that almost every day under 'The marriage has been arranged' in *The Times*, we recognize at least one couple as our clients.

This is why, right up until the 1990s, it was rare to come across those who successfully found love in this way. Almost all simply refused to admit it.

The first rumblings of a sexual revolution to be seen in the personal columns emanated from the gay community. In 1966, openly gay contact ads were published for the first time in the underground paper the *International Times*, an innovation for which it later faced prosecution. The legalisation of homosexuality in 1967 inspired a further flurry of opportunities. *Jeffrey*, launched in 1972 as one of Britain's original specialist gay magazines, featured contact ads from the beginning, as did the *Gay Times*, established in 1974. The latter saw the use of some of the genre's earliest abbreviations, such as 'A.L.A' (all letters answered); in every other way, however, the genre was not yet well established enough to boast a jargon of its own, and in this way the simplicity of the language employed – 'Man seeks man' – recalls some of the very earliest heterosexual ads. The same applies to the first ads from lesbians: 'Married lesbian lady wishes to meet similar, Brighton area' ran one in the feminist magazine *Spare Rib*.

By the end of the 1970s, gay ads were beginning to work their way into the more mainstream press. Thus, for the first time, the homosexual world occupied the same space – literally and figuratively – as the heterosexual one. In *Private Eye*, such ads were initially very occasional, just one every few issues: 'Gay loner, 35 (Jersey, C.I.), interested in history, old buildings, antiques, gardens, old cars, seeks friendship with intelligent, attractive man about 30.' But they rapidly became not only more common, but also more open about the fact that the focus was primarily on sex: 'Young man, attractive and intelligent, seeks gay relationships, photo optional, phone Steve . . .'

The heterosexual community also soon incorporated its new sexual freedoms into the sort of personal ads it placed. The first swingers' ads ('My husband and I wish to meet other attractive couples for broadminded friendship . . .') appeared in small-scale publications like *Exit* and *Way Out* – though both later faced prosecution as a result – and by the late 1960s about fifteen or sixteen magazines offered similar opportunities, one of which, *The Correspondent*, claimed to have 20,000 readers. By 1971 there were also swingers' ads in mainstream publications such as *Time Out*.

A year later, the number of marriages taking place in Britain hit an all-time peak of 480,285. With the invention of the Pill, the decade gave rise to the disentanglement once and for all of marriage and sex. This process had been in evidence since the likes of *Round-About* magazine in the 1890s, but culminated in the 1970s as the Lonely Hearts genre was reinvented in response to a huge shift in society's mores.

So, sprinkled among the many ads (often up to twenty or thirty an issue) from men offering to marry anyone in need of British citizenship, in return for cash payment (which curiously dominated the personal columns of *Private Eye* in the early 1970s), there were a number of Lonely Hearts ads that were typical of the period. The 1973 Royal Wedding souvenir edition (strapline: 'You're not losing a filly, you're gaining a stallion!') featured a '30 year old, free, handsome, businessman' who 'seeks young twenties girl for electric evenings. If compatible could live in. Phone Terry . . . after 8 evenings or weekends.' The men routinely used the terms 'chick' or 'bird' to refer to women, many seeking someone who was 'politically and sexually aware', others in search of 'extra-maritals', such as the business executive who was after an 'uninhibited girl with a view to interesting friendship unencumbered by tedium and the marriage contract'. By the middle of the decade, the ads appearing in the *New Statesman* were equally dubious: there was the university teacher in search of an 'intimate, enduring, discreet liaison with educated lady' and the forty-four-year-old Canadian lawyer, 'married but wife cannot travel', who 'seeks companionship of sophisticated, attractive, educated lady, not too high-brow, for holidays in Europe . . .'

Unsurprisingly, the ads that appeared in the feminist magazine *Spare Rib* struck a sexually liberated tone from the start: 'Inner-freedom-seeking, radical relationship wanted, aware woman friend sought by young, non-English bachelor guy, for awareness, sharing and sex.' There were male transvestites looking for permanent relationships with females, straight males looking for companionship and sex, and everything in between. One 1973 edition saw the gender wars played out on the letters page. An ad had appeared from a 'Gentleman, retired widower with nice house on South Coast' who was looking to contact a woman aged between thirty-five and forty with a 'keen sense of humour'. It prompted a furious letter from Marie Peyton of Winchester, who was, she wrote, 'both extremely disgusted and depressed' by the ad: 'By printing [it] you are encouraging old men to look for young women to take what could at best be a stupid action, at worst a tragic one.' She raged on:

> This sort of ad, and that attitude of mind behind it, fills doctors' surgeries with women of 40 years and over, divorcees and widows suffering from Depression which the doctor cannot cure because they find that once passed the age of 40 years they are considered 'sexually finished', and their sexual lives are over . . . I thought that the purpose of your magazine was to clear people's minds of the traditional prejudices against women, including middle-aged women surely?

But as the decade progressed, the highly conventional ad that featured an older man looking for a younger woman – traditionally the staple of the personal columns – temporarily disappeared from *Spare Rib*. The March 1977 edition ('Simone de Beauvoir interviewed,' trumpeted the cover) included an ad from a thirty-one-year-old man – 'ordinary sorta job, vegetarian, feminist, interested therapy, meditation, "growth movement"' – who sought a 'female for caring but unprogrammed relationship'. This was next to ads from, among others, a twenty-nine-year-old heterosexual, cross-dressing publishing executive, a commune in Shropshire, the feminist press Virago, and a number of family-planning services. It was a sign of the times.

It is noticeable, however, that in all the magazines of the period, even *Spare Rib*, the ads placed by men are far more permissive in tone than those placed by women, and far outnumber them. Perhaps the more sexually liberated women were too busy actually having sex to place an ad simply looking to do so. Instead, the ads from women tended to be rather dramatic in their demands: '£50 for temporary relationship resulting pregnancy,' ran one that appeared in *Private Eye* in 1973. It is certainly not a plea that would have appeared in the *Morning Chronicle* 200 years before. Those women who do seek a more conventional set-up are increasingly emotionally open about what it is that they require from a partner:

> I am thirty, female, and have quite a lot to offer, but I am lonely and unhappy. This is mainly because I seem unable to reconcile compulsive demands for security with the stifling of life which this involves. Is there a man who perhaps shares my love of music and of walking, and who might have the wisdom and patience to help me find the way through my dilemma (preferably in the Hereford Area)?

This ad appeared in the *New Statesman* in 1976, alongside another from a 'Swiss count's daughter, 27, Christian, lively, beautiful, intd. arts', which proves that it is actually all but impossible to generalise about the sort of people who placed ads; she 'sks very refined yng man. Oxon/Cantab. No sex!'

By the 1980s, both the *New Statesman* and *Private Eye* featured about thirty Lonely Hearts ads an issue, some of which received up to 150 replies each. Most were pretty straightforward and read similarly to those today. 'Non-smoking' was a common demand, and it had become rare to mention money outright, though some did employ euphemisms such as 'home-owning' to the same effect. Thus, compared to the 1780s, there was evidence in the personal columns of a far less robust attitude to the economics of marriage, which is ironic in view of the fact that the 1980s are commonly seen as a decade when money ruled. The well-known abbreviation G.S.O.H. (good sense of humour) emerged in the late 1980s, as did W.L.T.M. (would like to meet). A far greater number of people, however, continued to turn to agencies rather than ads for help in finding love.

And then came the Internet.

An awful lot has been written about the rise of Lonely Hearts ads on the Internet. Every week the Sunday papers seem to feature some story about how five million people in the UK alone are looking for love online. The Internet has, for the first time, made Lonely Hearts ads an (almost) mainstream option. Almost all my single friends are currently engaged at some level or another in Internet dating, and rarely does a Sunday brunch go by without being regaled with tales of the latest disastrous date (as well as the occasional successful one); one couple who met this way have just invited me to their wedding next Christmas. Advertising for love is now an essential tool in the modern courtship process. The phenomenon that sociologist Anthony Giddens has termed 'the commodification of the self in late modernity' – that is, the idea that every aspect of modern life has been penetrated by commercial practices – is one that very much applies in this context. Ours is an age of rampant consumerism, which has trained us to have the highest of expectations. We do not just want the best car, the best designer bag, the best sunglasses – we also want the 'best' spouse. In an age that is all about 'sell, sell, sell', it is no wonder that it has become increasingly acceptable to sell ourselves.

*

Over the past three centuries, Lonely Hearts ads have consistently reflected the same central – and, to many of us, dispiriting – truth that has also been identified in almost every recent study of human courtship: men seek youth and offer financial security, while for women it is precisely the other way round.

The reason men seek youth (along with its cue, physical attractiveness) is because in evolutionary terms it is an indication of fertility – that is, of the ability to provide fit, healthy children for many years to come. Thus from her late twenties onwards a woman's 'value' on the marriage market declines, for the simple reason that so does her fertility. Correspondingly, a constant of Lonely Hearts ads since their earliest days has been the search for a wife who is 'young', ideally between twenty and thirty. Similarly, terms like 'healthy', a 'good physiognomy' or 'a pleasing figure' have functioned as catch-all phrases for someone with an odds-on chance of reproductive success.

Women, on the other hand, have historically not been in a position to be choosy. They just wanted a husband – any husband – as long as he fulfilled the one evolutionary preference that the female sex has consistently sought to implement: he must possess the means to support and feed their offspring ('income', 'property' or a 'fortune', in the lexicon of the ads).

Ads placed in the 1990s and 2000s, however, reveal a small but significant shift in these evolutionary preferences. Now that women are able to have children so much later in life, youth is no longer the be-all and end-all for men when choosing a partner (though physical attractiveness remains their sole most important criteria by far, studies show). And for women financial security is not such a

priority now, not only due to the increase in their earning potential, but also because of the rise in voluntary childlessness. Women
are becoming pickier too, typically demanding that their opposite
numbers meet a far longer list of criteria than they once did. Thus
it may be that the traditional rules that have dictated human mate
choice – the trade-off of youth for money – will become decreas-
ingly rigid, the further we move into the twenty-first century.

In terms of the circumstances in which a Lonely Hearts ad is
placed, for men these have remained remarkably constant: they work
too hard, they are new in town, it is hard to meet new people. For
women, however, they have changed dramatically. Where once it was
the last resort of only the truly tragic (remember Eleanora in 1788
or Ada in 1882), today it is just one of a multitude of options.
More women now place Lonely Hearts ads then men (most studies
put the figure at about 60 per cent), which is a major turnaround.
Their ads are no longer like 'Brechtian texts, with all of society
milling around', but instead more akin to 'Beckettian texts, where
individuals are revealed in isolation'. The emphasis has shifted away
from family and community and towards a highly developed sense
of individualism. One unfortunate side-effect of this is that it is
now women as much as (if not more than) men who use Lonely
Hearts ads for criminal purposes, in particular to perpetrate fraud.

Lonely Hearts ads of every era have demonstrated distinct stylistic
conventions, with the result that many end up sharing a common
language and structure. Twenty-first-century ads tend to distinguish
themselves with the ubiquitous use of abbreviations. Terms like
'W.L.T.M.' or 'G.S.O.H.' have become an accepted element of everyday
parlance, reflecting just how widespread such ads have become. After
a while, however, all the advertisers start to sound the same, which
is perhaps the intention: by reducing one's identity to forty words
of (mostly predictable) adjectives, one portrays oneself as Everyman
or Everywoman, thereby avoiding the risk of sounding silly. There
have always been exceptions to this rule – those who consciously

seek to stand out from the crowd (just browse the ads in any edition of the *London Review of Books*) – but they are in the minority.

With Internet ads, which tend not to be charged by the word, space constraints no longer apply. Whether the resulting increase in both the number and length of ads has made it any easier to track down the perfect partner is, however, debatable. Dating websites tend to be a bit overwhelming, making it *more* difficult to choose between the prospective candidates, rather than less. On a positive note, though, longer ads have resulted in a broader range of self-representation that moves beyond traditional stereotypes of what is deemed attractive. Thus with the looks-for-money exchange no longer dominating courtship to the extent it once did, the dating world has, in gender terms, become a little more equal.

While Lonely Hearts ads have reflected a clear and significant rise in sexual permissiveness in recent years, it remains the case that the huge majority of those who advertise are in search of a serious relationship. Ours is a surprisingly conventional generation in this respect. For although over the past twenty-five years the number of marriages has dropped by 30 per cent, falling in 2008 to an all-time low of 232,990 (with the mean age of first marriage increasing accordingly, to 32.1 years for men and 29.9 years for women), what is more surprising is that the institution of marriage has managed to survive at all. Someone to spend one's whole life with, to share a bathroom with, to roll around naked with 2.4 times a week (if the statistics are to be believed), every single week, for ever and ever? It is plainly a preposterous proposition, yet one that has endured to an astonishing degree. There are numerous possible reasons for this (wanting to commit for the sake of the children, economic strictures, legal benefits, the desire to rebel against our parents, who were the very generation who fought for the right not to have to settle down); but, above all else, what our continuing enthusiasm for marriage exposes is the powerful streak of optimism that resides within many of us. It is the voice in one's head that declares, 'My marriage will be the one that works – oh yes, it will', thereby wilfully disregarding the oft-quoted statistic that nearly half of all marriages end in divorce. (And, to be fair, divorce rates have fallen recently, and in 2008 they were the lowest they have been in twenty-nine years.)

And so it is that Lonely Hearts ads are still with us: more prolific, often more explicit and arguably more successful than ever before – a bold statement in black ink, or more often black type, of how society has changed. They are a public declaration of the most human of desires, love and companionship, desires that in the twenty-first century are as pronounced as ever, as the battle intensifies against what Karl Marx termed 'alienation'. There will always be those who are willing to do whatever it takes to track down their perfect partner. And rightly so. For Lonely Hearts ads are, in essence, just an expression of hope. And without hope, what else is there?

Notes and Further Reading

The majority of the material contained in this book is based on primary research conducted in the British Library's newspaper reading room in Colindale, as well as via its digitised newspaper collection, which is increasing in size and scope with each year that passes. Other digitised collections such as *The Times Digital Archive* or *Eighteenth Century Collections Online* are also widely accessible simply with a local library card. Where no reference is provided for an ad either in the text or in the notes below, the source is *Matrimonial Advertisements* (1846), a scrapbook held in the British Library at St Pancras. It has no page numbers and does not always give sources, but is nonetheless an invaluable resource of late eighteenth- and early nineteenth-century Lonely Hearts ads.

In terms of secondary sources, surprisingly few books have been written about the history of courtship and marriage. The most useful was John R. Gillis, *For Better, For Worse: British Marriages, 1600 to the present* (1985), but others that were also consulted include Alan Macfarlane, *Marriage and Love in England 1300–1840* (1986); Lawrence Stone, *Uncertain Unions and Broken Lives: Marriage and Divorce in England, 1660–1857* (1995); and Stephanie Coontz, *Marriage: A history* (2005).

Chapter One: Nine Days Wonder and Laughter

There is a 1969 facsimile of John Houghton's *A Collection for Improvement of Husbandry and Trade*, from which all quotes are taken. *The Tatler*, 14 September 1710, is the source of the phrase 'Accounts of News from the little World'. Other publications referred to in this chapter are *Athenian*

Mercury, 6 May 1694; *Mercurius Fumigosus*, 16 May 1660; *Mercurius Publicus*, 28 June 1660; *Poor Robin's Intelligence*, 17 October 1676; *Mercurius Matrimonialis; or, Chapmen for the Ladies Lately Offered to Sale by Way of Auction*, July 1691; and *A Catalogue of Ladies*, August 1691. Books and articles that provided background information include: Helen Berry, *Gender, society and print culture in late-Stuart England: The cultural world of the Athenian Mercury* (2003); Richard Adair, *Courtship, illegitimacy and marriage in early modern England* (1996); David M. Turner, *Fashioning adultery: Gender, sex and civility in England, 1660–1740* (2002); David Cressy, *Literacy and the social order: Reading and writing in Tudor and Stuart England* (1980); Joseph Frank, *The Beginnings of the English Newspaper, 1620–1660* (1961); and E.S. De Beer, 'The English Newspaper from 1695–1702' in Ragnhild Hatton and J.S. Bromley (eds), *William III and Louis XIV: Essays 1680–1720* (1968).

Chapter Two: A Want of Acquaintance

Britain's first 'Once Seen' ad appeared in *The Tatler*, 21 March 1709, while the letter that offered help was in the 23 September 1710 edition. Samuel Johnson commented on the subject in *The Idler*, 1 July 1758. Jeremy Black, *The English Press in the Eighteenth Century* (1987), quotes a 1736 edition of *Fog's Weekly Journal* on 'pieces of *domestic* intelligence' and a 1725 edition of *Mist's Weekly Journal* on 'a great and populous City like this'. Also useful was an article by A. Bruttini entitled 'Advertising and Socio-economic transformations in England 1720–1760' in the *Journal of Advertising History* (1928) Vol. 5. The gentleman 'of a vigorous, strong, and amorous constitution' is from the *Daily Advertiser* as quoted in the *Gentleman's Magazine*, May 1750, as is the one in search of a wife with 'good teeth, soft lips, sweet breath'. The 'agreeable young gentleman in trade' featured in the *Daily Advertiser*, 11 October 1750; the *Cambridge Journal* ad is from the 15 March 1746 edition. The letter to the *Lady's Magazine* was published in September 1759, while the *Gentleman's Magazine* satirised the genre in March and April 1740. The 'Once Seen' ads quoted towards the end of the chapter are mostly from an anonymous anthology of ads entitled *Love at First Sight*

(1750), as well as from the *General Advertiser*, 30 March 1748; *London Chronicle*, 5 August 1758; and *Daily Advertiser*, 6 May 1759.

Chapter Three: A Feeling Heart

Isaac Bickerstaffe imagined the scene in his play, *Love in the City* (1767). Coffee-houses are described in Brian Cowan, *The Social Life of Coffee: the emergence of the British coffeehouse* (2005). The recent scholarship on marriage is Stephanie Coontz, *Marriage: A History* (2005).

The man in search of a wife to 'sit by a genteel fire-side' is in the *Public Ledger*, 2 February 1769. Roy Porter, *English Society in the Eighteenth Century* (1990) is the source of the Mrs Montagu quote. The attempt to replace a servant with a wife is in the *Daily Advertiser*, 14 September 1770. B. Pawlowski and R.I.M. Dunbar, 'Impact of market value on human mate choice decisions' in *Proceedings of the Royal Society of London* (1999), 266, found social skills to be a top priority in mate choice. The *Norwich Mercury* ad is from the 4 March 1769 edition.

The disadvantages of 'delicacy' for women are discussed in G.J. Barker-Benfield, *The Culture of Sensibility: Sex and society in eighteenth-century Britain* (1992). Some of the quotes used in this chapter are to be found there too. The Patricia Meyer Spacks quote is from her book *Novel Beginnings: Experiments in eighteenth-century English fiction* (2006).

A 'widow in business' is sought in the *Daily Advertiser*, 13 September 1769, while the despairing bachelor is in the *Morning Post*, 5 July 1777. The ad in the *Ledger* in the summer of 1769 appeared on 11 August and Johnson joked in *The Idler*, 1 July, 1758. For *Aris's Gazette*, see J.A. Langford, *A Century of Birmingham Life: or, a chronicle of local events from 1741 to 1841* (1868). It is Bickerstaffe in his *Love in the City* again, who compares marriage to a mouse trap. The 'reputable tradesman' and Timothy Surrell advertised in the *Morning Chronicle*, 19 July 1794 and the *Reading Mercury*, 18 September 1798, respectively.

The quote from John Walter is from the first edition of *The Times*, 1 January 1785. The 'Burnt Lady' was featured on 17 and 31 October 1786;

the reference to the ostrich was on 11 December 1786. Alice Clay, *The Agony Column of* The Times *1800–1870* (1881), and Stephen Winkworth, *Room Two More Guns: An intriguing history of the personal column of* The Times (1986), were also helpful for this and subsequent chapters. Finally, the letters to the *Edinburgh Courant* are reprinted in William Creech (ed.), *Edinburgh Fugitive Pieces* (1791).

Chapter Four: Sighs and Lamentations

The principal source of background material for this chapter was G.J. Barker-Benfield's brilliant book *The Culture of Sensibility: Sex and society in eighteenth-century Britain* (1992), from which a number of the ideas and quotes are drawn. Also helpful was Bridget Hill, *Women Alone: Spinsters in England, 1660–1850* (2001).

The quote from Lady Mary Wortley Montagu is in Vol. 1 of Robert Halsband (ed.), *The Complete Letters of Lady Mary Wortley Montagu*. Mary Warde is mentioned by Amanda Vickery in *The Gentleman's Daughter: Women's lives in Georgian England* (1998), which also contains an interesting discussion of why wealthy women increasingly found themselves with time to read. For *Aris's Gazette*, see Langford, *Birmingham Life*.

On the novel in the eighteenth century, see J. Paul Hunter, *Before Novels: The cultural contexts of eighteenth-century English fiction* (1990); David Cressy, *Literacy and the social order: Reading and writing in Tudor and Stuart England* (1980); J.M.S. Tompkins, *The Popular Novel in England, 1770–1800* (1969); and Jill Campbell, 'Domestic intelligence: Newspaper advertising and the eighteenth-century novel' in *Yale Journal of Criticism* (2002). For women's relationship with the novel specifically, see Janet Todd, *Sensibility: An introduction* (1986); Patricia Meyer Spacks, *Privacy: Concealing the eighteenth-century self* (2003); and Vic Gatrell, *City of Laughter: Sex and Satire in eighteenth-century London* (2006).

For the play by Sarah Gardner, see Isobel Grundy, 'Sarah Gardner: "Such Trumpery" or "A Lustre to her Sex"?' in *Tulsa Studies in Women's Literature* (1988). Andrea Bradley's 2005 PhD dissertation at Vanderbilt University entitled 'Wanted: Advertising in British Literature, 1700–1830' was also consulted.

The quote about 'simultaneous self-assertion and self-concealment' is from Patricia Meyer Spacks, *Privacy*. Age is discussed in an article by B. Pawlowski and R.I.M. Dunbar entitled 'Withholding Age as Putative Deception in Mate Search Tactics' in *Evolution and Human Behaviour* (1999), and the effect of the French Revolution on Lonely Hearts ads is noted in Jennifer M. Jones, 'Personals and Politics: Courting la "citoyenne" in "Le courier de l'hymen"' in *Yale French Studies* (2001). The widow in *The Times* in search of a man who does not drink too much claret is in the edition of 25 May 1787.

The widow's ad in the *Public Advertiser* is in the 18 November 1768 edition, while Kitty Fisher appeared in the same paper on 30 March 1759, as did the MP on 16 April 1776.

Chapter Five: Enterprizing Enamoratos

Sir John Dineley's various antics are recounted in the *Oxford Dictionary of National Biography*; John Timbs, *English Eccentrics* (1877); and Charles Kingston, *The Marriage Market* (1926). All quotes from Johann Wilhelm von D'Archenholz can be found in Vol. 1 of his *A Picture of England* (1789). 'Quack medicine' is mentioned in Prince Hoare's play *Indiscretion* (1800), and 'R.R.' advertised in the *Daily Advertiser*, 12 March 1777.

The Robert Southey quotes about ads are taken from the 1984 edition of his *Letters from England* (1807), edited by J. Simmons. The warning from the *Matrimonial Magazine* appeared on the first page of the first edition, which was published in 1775. The 'Gentleman of Honour and Property' advertised himself in the *Morning Post*, 21 January 1775, and the 'lady swerves' in *The Matrimonial Advertisement* by Sarah Gardner, quoted in Grundy, 'Sarah Gardner'. 'Without fear or intimidation' is the reassurance given in *The Times*, 4 March 1795. John Bowdler and Robert Southey are quoted in Ben Wilson's *Decency and Disorder: the age of cant, 1789–1837* (2007), which was also a useful source of background information for this chapter. A 'secret in the newspaper' is from George Colman's play *X.Y.Z.* (1820). M.G. Anderson writes about 'the meanings of marriage' in *Negotiating Marriage: Female playwrights and eighteenth-century comedy* (2002).

The hoax was reported in the 29 August 1825 edition of the *Morning Chronicle*. For another excellent example, see *The Times*, 20 August 1824, which recounts how an ad appeared in one of the London morning papers from a surgeon looking for a wife who possessed a fortune sufficient to help fund his dream of establishing his own practice. The ad was answered by a young wag living in Bridgwater, leading to all sorts of tomfoolery. 'It is to be hoped that this will be a lesson to him for the future, and teach him that the ladies of Somerset are not so prodigal of their fortunes and personal attractions as to be duped by the schemes of a speculating Cockney,' commented the *Taunton Courier*.

The Dover Street agency is discussed in Henry Sampson, *History of Advertising* (1874); see also the *Morning Post*, 17 October 1776. The masked ball at Carlisle House was reported in the *Gentleman's Magazine*, 16 July 1776. Information on the Imprejudicate Nuptial Society can be found in the anonymous pamphlet *Matrimonial Plan* (1795); on the New Matrimonial Plan in Sampson, *Advertising*, and on the Imperial Matrimonial Association in *The Times*, 16 December 1825. Ads from *Galignani's* were reprinted in *The Times*, 8 September 1826. Byron wrote about them in a letter of 30 September 1812, which can be found in Vol. II of the collection of his letters and journals edited by Leslie A. Marchand. Lord Lucan's ad is quoted in Sampson, *Advertising*.

Chapter Six: A Private Gentleman

The best source for the Red Barn murder is *The Times*, 8, 9, 11 and 12 August 1828, and all quotes in this chapter are from there, unless otherwise stated. The local magistrate is referenced in J. Curtis, *The Murder of Maria Marten*, ed. Jeanne and Norman Mackenzie (1948). All the letters to Corder from potential wives can be found in George Foster, *An Accurate Account of the Trial of William Corder for the Murder of Maria Marten . . .* (1828). The detail that Corder was making boiled eggs when he was arrested is from *John Bull Magazine*, 27 April 1828. Thomas Hardy mentions the trial in William Greenslade (ed.), *Thomas Hardy's 'Facts' Notebook* (2004); see also the *Dorset County Chronicle*, 1 May 1828 and 14 August 1828. The quote about 'a melo-dramatic romance' is from Knight and Lacey, *The Trials of William Corder* (1828). For the 'age of cant', see Vic Gatrell, *City of Laughter* (2006); Ben Wilson, *Decency and Disorder* (2007); and Boyd Hilton, *A Mad, Bad, & Dangerous People? England 1783–1846* (2006). The quote about 'speculative, sensual and sordid men' is from J. Curtis, *Maria Marten*, as is the one about 'the trash of a Matrimonial Advertisement'. 'Maiden modesty' is from Foster, *William Corder*. Martin J. Wiener's *Men of Blood: Violence, manliness and criminal justice in Victorian England* (2004) is also relevant.

Chapter Seven: Puffs for Adventurers

On 'prudery', see Vic Gatrell, *City of Laughter* (2006); Ben Wilson, *Decency and Disorder* (2007); and Boyd Hilton, *Mad, Bad, & Dangerous* (2006). The *Fraser's* article was in the April 1835 edition of the magazine. The letter to the *Bristol Mercury* was printed on 1 July 1837. For more examples of ads from working-class men, see the *Belfast News-Letter*, 9 September 1828, and *The Times*, 2 February 1837. The *Leeds Mercury* weighed in on the subject on 7 January 1864 and Baron von Hallberg de Broech's ad was reprinted in *The Times* on 15 January 1841.

Flora Tristan's comment is from the 1980 edition of her *London Journal* and John Stuart Mill is quoted in Marjorie Morgan, *Manners, Morals and Class in England, 1774–1858* (1994). The letter appeared in the *Leeds Mercury* on 7 January 1864, and the 'cart before a horse' was reported in the *Belfast News-Letter*, 18 May 1864.

Charlotte Brontë's short story 'Henry Hastings' is available in *Five Novelettes*, ed. Winifred Gerin (1971). The letter from Brontë to Nussey is dated 5 March 1839, and is reprinted in Vol. 1 of *The Letters of Charlotte Brontë*, ed. Margaret Smith. For *Aris's Gazette*, see Langford, *Birmingham Life*.

The two hoaxes in *The Times* were reported on 23 July 1830 and 14 November 1837. For more examples like these, see the *Morning Chronicle*, 5 November 1828; *Hull Packet and East Riding Times*, 22 August 1845; *Manchester*

Times, 27 February 1849; *Morning Chronicle*, 17 September 1852; *Reynolds's Newspaper*, 15 February 1857; *Western Mail*, 28 May 1869; *Hull Packet and East Riding Times*, 7 May 1869.

The number of newspapers in existence was calculated with the assistance of the bibliography to the *Cambridge History of English and American Literature*, Vol. 14, *The Victorian Age*, Part Two, IV, 'The Growth of Journalism'. On advertising in this period, see T.R. Nevett, *Advertising in Britain: A history* (1982). *Punch* is quoted in Morgan, *Manners*. The 'unlucky man' was in the *Leeds Mercury*, 23 September 1843, and the Tyneside man was in *The Times*, 11 February 1857. *Reynolds's Newspaper* commented on the subject on 15 February 1857, as did *Vanity Fair* on 11 August 1860. The man with a predilection for one-legged women advertised in the *Shoreditch Observer*, 11 July 1863, reprinted in (among other places) the *Bristol Mercury*, 18 July 1863, and the *Liverpool Mercury*, 21 July 1863.

Chapter Eight: The Tomfoolery of Silly Girls

Ada Milne's predicament is recounted in *The Times*, 12 October 1882 and *Birmingham Daily Post*, 12 October 1882; see also the UK censuses of 1881 and 1891. The 'English gentleman, practising abroad' and the thirty-year-old lawyer appear in *Matrimonial News*, 2 January 1880 and 1 May 1875, respectively. 'Blanche and Lily' are discussed in the *Pall Mall Gazette*, 18 December 1871. Mary Paley Marshall is quoted in Pat Jalland, *Women, Marriage and Politics, 1860–1914* (1986). The *Leeds Mercury* commented on the subject in the 7 January 1864 edition, and 'Lilian, Gladys and Rosalie' advertised themselves in *Matrimonial News*, 19 December 1875. The relationship between women and shopping generally is discussed in Erika Diane Rappaport, *Shopping for Pleasure: Women in the making of London's West End* (2000); Lori Anne Loeb, *Consuming Angels: Advertising and Victorian women* (1994); Judith R. Walkowitz, *City of Dreadful Delight: Narratives of sexual danger in late-Victorian London* (1992); and Lucy Bland, *Banishing the Beast: English Feminism and Sexual Morality, 1885–1914* (1995).

The comments of the *Daily News* are in the 3 May 1877 edition, and of the *Pall Mall Gazette* in the 7 March 1878 edition. The young Russian nobleman featured in *Cupid's Cosmopolitan Carrier* in September 1888. The first edition of the *Matrimonial Herald*, which was originally called *Nuptials*, appeared on 12 January 1884. It called itself a 'Rocket' on 6 September 1884.

The rise of marriage rates, as well as the Flora Thompson quote, is drawn from Gillis, *For Better, For Worse*. The research about how working-class girls met their knight in shining armour is in F. Barret-Ducrocq, *Love in the Time of Victoria: Sexuality, class and gender in nineteenth-century London* (1991) and Ginger S. Frost, *Promises Broken: Courtship, class and gender in Victorian England* (1995), both of which are excellent and unusual texts on courtship in this period, a subject that has thus far received surprisingly little academic attention.

The *Pall Mall Gazette*'s comments about matrimonial journals were published on 5 September 1888, which is also when it revealed that many doubled as marriage agencies. *The Sun*'s investigation ran in the 27 July 1893 edition. The dodgy ads from the *Matrimonial Post* appeared on 10 October 1891. For more examples of breach-of-promise cases arising from Lonely Hearts ads, see *The Graphic*, 18 March 1876; *Manchester Examiner and Times*, 28 February 1889; and *Birmingham Daily Post*, 2 March 1889.

The Knowles/Duncan case was reported in *The Times*, 13 August 1890, and *Manchester Times*, 15 August 1890. The *Matrimonial Herald* case was reported in *The Times*, 12, 19 and 26 November 1895; 3, 18, 23, 24 and 31 December 1895; January 1, 8, 11, 14 and 29, 1896; 29 February 1896; and 2, 3, 4, 5, 6, and 7 March 1896. See also *Return of Working of Regulations for carrying out Prosecution of Offences Acts, 1895* (1896), and the UK census of 1901. Analysis of the case, as well as more information, can be found in Angus McLaren, *The Trials of Masculinity: Policing sexual boundaries, 1870–1930* (1997).

The case of Hannah Tring was reported in *Reynolds's Newspaper*, 2 December 1894, and *Western Mail*, 30 November 1894; see also the UK census of 1891. Horace Tulle's fraud appeared in *Lloyd's Weekly Newspaper*, 15 October 1899. Frederick Hall's fraud was in *The Times*, 28 November 1900; see also *Return of Working of Regulations made in 1886 for carrying out Prosecution* of *Offences Acts, 1879 and 1884* (1901). For more examples of cases of financial fraud arising from Lonely Hearts ads, see *The Times*, 15 June 1877; *Western Mail*, 14 June 1877; *Plymouth and Cornish Advertiser*, 19 March 892; *Birmingham Daily Post*, 21 February 1894; *Birmingham Daily Post*, 21 January 1895; and *Return of Working of Regulations for carrying out Prosecution of Offences Acts, 1894* (1895).

Evans Wood's identity fraud was widely reported, including in the *New York Times*, 17 August 1898 and 6 April 1900; *Newcastle Weekly Courant*, 3 and 17 March 1900; and *Birmingham Daily Post*, 13 March 1900. The women involved were morally censured in *The Times*, 26 July 1893 and *Reynolds's Newspaper*, 3 July 1898.

Other useful sources of background information for this chapter included Lucy Brown, *News and Newspapers in Victorian England* (1985); Joan Perkin, *Women and Marriage in nineteenth-century England* (1988); Jeffrey Weeks, *Sex, Politics and Society: the regulation of sexuality since 1800* (1989); and Michael Wolff and H.J. Dyos, *The Victorian City: Images and Realities* (1999).

Chapter Nine: A True Comrade and Friend

A significant proportion of Chapter Nine is based upon the research of H.G. Cocks. See his articles '"Sporty" Girls and "Artistic" Boys: Friendship, Illicit Sex, and the British "Companionship" Advertisement, 1913–1922?' in *Journal of the History of Sexuality* (2002), and 'Peril in the Personals: The dangers and pleasures of classified advertising in early twentieth-century Britain' in *Media History* (2004), as well as his recent book *Classified: The secret history of the personal column* (2009). Other books and articles that provided crucial information are Claire Langhamer, 'Love and Courtship in mid-twentieth century England' in *Historical Journal* (2007); Virginia Nicholson, *Singled Out: How two million women survived without men after the First World War* (2007); Ruth Adam, *A Woman's Place* (reprinted in 2000); G.R. Searle, *A New England? Peace and war, 1886–1918* (2005); and Nicola Beauman's pioneering work, *A Very Great Profession: The Woman's Novel, 1914–1939* (reprinted in 2008).

Sincere thanks to Kath Boothman, who got in touch with the author about her grandparents, Jack and Gertie. The quotes about sexual liberation are from Coontz, *Marriage*. Editions of *Round-About* quoted are 15 July 1898 and 15 May 1899. For the trial of Frank and Edith Jackson, see *The Times*, 11 October and 21 December 1901. Cicily Hamilton's comment on marriage is in her book, *Marriage as a Trade* (1909). The case of Gerald Fitzgerald was reported in *The Times*, 2 and 9 October and 8 November 1915; for similar cases, see *The Times*, 30 April 1917 and 20 June 1918. Vera Brittain's view of ads can be found in her 1933 memoir *Testament of Youth*. The case of Charlie Clarkson and Beatrice Pimm featured in *The Times*, 8 November 1923; see also the UK census of 1921. George Orwell is quoted in McLaren, *Trials of Masculinity*.

For other interesting criminal cases involving Lonely Hearts ads in this period, see *The Times*, 29 March 1904; 3 June 1904; 10 November 1908; 16 May 1911; 5 July 1911; 14 June 1912; 27 January 1913; 29 June 1929; and 2 July 1934.

Chapter Ten: Electric Evenings

Lady (Sarah) Burns was enormously generous and helpful in recounting to the author her experiences at *Private Eye*. Eleanor Radford's interview with the *Evening Star* is quoted in the 1961 volume of the *Matrimonial Times*. Marriage in general in the 1950s is discussed in Gillis, *For Better, For Worse*; Langhamer, 'Love and Courtship'; and Marcus Collins, *Modern Love: an intimate history of men and women in twentieth-century Britain* (2003). David Kynaston's marvellous book *Austerity Britain* (2008) also provided thought-provoking background information about the *mentalité* of these years. Heather Jenner writes of her experiences in her books *Marriage is My Business* (1953) and *The Marriage Book* (1964); the author also received a fascinating email on the subject from a former researcher for the Consumers' Association.

The advent of gay ads and swingers' ads is discussed in Cocks, *Classified*. The *Spare Rib* ads quoted in this chapter are from the editions of March 1973, November 1973 and March 1977. The *Private Eye* ads are from the editions of 29 June 1973; 16 November 1973; 17 August 1979; 21 December 1979; 24 April 1981; and 20 March 1987. The *New Statesman* ads are from the editions of 5 March 1960, and 25 June 1976.

How Giddens' theory of 'the commodification of the self' relates to Lonely Hearts ads is discussed in Justine Coupland, 'Dating Advertisements: Discourses of the commodified self' in *Discourse and Society* (1996). The decline of a woman's 'value' in relation to her fertility is analysed in Pawlowski and Dunbar, 'Impact of Market Value'. The evidence that women are becoming increasingly choosy is in Louise Barrett, Robin Dunbar and John Lycett, *Human Evolutionary Psychology* (2002), and the quote about 'Beckettian texts' is from Rukmini Bhaya Nair, 'Gender, Genre and Generative Grammar: deconstructing the matrimonial column', in Michael Toolan (ed.), *Language, Text and Context: Essays in Stylistics* (1992). For an entertaining overview of some of the more unusual ads of recent times, see David Rose, *They Call Me Naughty Lola: Personal ads from the London Review of Books* (2006).

There is a huge body of fascinating literature on the theory of modern Lonely Hearts ads. Highlights include Robert Kurzban and Jason Weeden, 'HurrayDate: Mate preferences in action' in *Evolution and Human Behavior* (2005), 26; David M. Buss, *The Evolution of Desire: Strategies of human mating* (2003); Mark Johnson, 'Partner Search: Presentation and representation', University of Oxford MSc Sociology Thesis (2003); Louise Barrett, Robin Dunbar and John Lycett, *Human Evolutionary Psychology* (2002), pp.93–101; Elizabeth Jagger, 'Marketing Molly and Melville: Dating in a postmodern society' in *Sociology* (2001), 35; Ranna Parekh, MD and Eugene V. Beresin, MD, 'Looking for Love? Take a cross-cultural walk through the personals' in *Academic Psychiatry* (2001), 25; John Cartwright, *Evolution and human behaviour: Darwinian perspectives on Human Nature* (2000); B. Pawlowski and R.I.M. Dunbar, 'Impact of market value on human mate choice decisions' in *Proceedings of the Royal Society of London* (1999), 266; B. Pawlowski and R.I.M. Dunbar, 'Withholding Age as Putative Deception in Mate Search Tactics' in *Evolution and Human Behaviour* (1999), 20; T. Bereczkei, S. Voros, A. Gal and L. Bernath, 'Resources, attractiveness, family commitment: Reproductive decisions in human mate choice' in *Ethology* (1997), 103; Justine Coupland, 'Dating Advertisements: Discourses of the commodified self' in *Discourse and Society* (1996); Paul Bruthiaux, *The Discourse of Classified Advertising* (1996); T. Bereczkei and A. Csanaky, 'Mate choice, marital success, and reproduction in a modern society' in *Ethology and Sociobiology* (1996), 17; D. Waynforth and R.I.M. Dunbar, 'Conditional mate choice strategies in humans: Evidence from "lonely hearts" advertisements' in *Behaviour* (1995), 132; P.P.G. Bateson (ed.), *Mate Choice* (1993); Simon Davis, 'Men as success objects and women as sex objects: A study of personal advertisements' in *Sex Roles* (1990), 23; David M. Buss, 'Sex differences in human mate preferences: evolutionary hypotheses tested in 37 cultures' in *Behavioral and Brain Sciences* (1989), 12; and Jeffrey L. Crane and Joy Michie Ino, 'A Discourse of Despair: The Semiology of Lonely-Hearts Language' in *Sociological Perspectives* (1987) 30. More recently there has also been a considerable amount of academic research into Internet dating, although – just like the newspaper investigations of a hundred years ago – almost all of it tends to focus on issues of deception. Finally, for recent examples of women committing Lonely Hearts fraud, see *The Guardian*, 31 January 2007; *The Times*, 23 June 2007; *Daily Telegraph*, 16 November 2009. And the figures on marriage and divorce are from the Office of National Statistics.

Index

Italic page numbers refer to illustrations

abbreviations (used in ads) 37, 179, 186, 190, 192
Adams, Daisy 164
Addison, Joseph 14
advertising, rise of 2–3, 7–9, 15, 124, 155–6
agony columns 6
Albert, Prince 118, 121
American Revolution 24, 33, 79, 81
Aris's Gazette 36, 50, 61, 122
Aristocratic Matrimonial & Marriage Envoy 133, 136
Athenian Mercury 6, 51
Austen, Jane 50, 51
    Pride and Prejudice 61
    Sense and Sensibility 56, 59

Barrett, Alfred 175, 176
Bason, George 147–8, 149
Beauty in Search of Knowledge (print) 66–7
Belasyse, Lady Elizabeth (later Countess of Lucan) 87
Benedict XVI, Pope 169
Bickerstaffe, Isaac, Love in the City 25–6, 79
bigamy 153, 167, 178

Binns, Edmund 126–7
Birks, Walter 175
Birmingham 36, 55
    Aris's Gazette 36, 50, 61, 122
birth control 161, 187
Blackwood's Magazine 119
Bone, Henry 88
Boothman, Kath 157, 159, 160
box-numbers 124, 181
Braddon, Mary, Lady Audley's Secret ix, 114
breach-of-promise 141–4
Bristol 115–16, 137, 168
Bristol Mercury 115, 139
Brittain, Vera 168
Brontë family 43, 119–20
Brontë, Charlotte, 'Henry Hastings' 120
Bunbury, Henry, The Coffee House 25
Burney, Fanny, Evelina 51–2, 57
Burnicle, John 157–60, 159
Burns, Sarah, Lady 181–2
Bury St Edmunds 102, 103–4
Byron, Robert, 6th Baron 87, 90

Cage-Birds (newspaper) 178
Cambridge Journal 18
cameras 139

Caroline of Brunswick (*later* Queen
    Caroline) vii
cartes de visite 139
Centlivre, Susanna, *A Bold Stroke for a
    Wife* 37
chaperones 109, 110, 178
Charles I, King (*earlier* Prince of
    Wales) 7–8
Charles II, King 8, 9
Charlotte, Queen 27
China viii
cinemas 172–3, *174*, 178
civil war, English 60–61
Clarkson, Charlie 169–70
coffee-houses vii, 11, 17, 21, 24, 25,
    43, 44, 65
*Collection for Improvement of Husbandry
    and Trade* (pamphlet) 2–3, 10, 11,
    14
Colman, George, *X.Y.Z.* 82
common-law marriage 136
companionship and friendship ads
    161, 173–5, 180
Congreve, William 7, 11
consumerism 29, 190–91
Consumers' Association 185
contraception 161, 187
Corder, William 90–106, *91*, *95*, *102*,
    108, 109, 112, 117
Correspondent, The (magazine) 187
costs of placing ads 50, 127
courtesans 62–3
cults 163–4
Cupid's Cosmopolitan Carrier 133
Curtis, J., *The Murder of Maria Marten*
    91, *92*, *94*, *102*, *104*, 106

Daily Advertiser 15, 16–17, 18, 20, 29,
    32, 59, 60, 73, 83
Daily Courant 14

Daily Express 173
Daily Mail 167, 169
Daily Mirror 173
Daily News 133
Daily Telegraph 124, 185
dance halls 178, 183
D'Archenholz, Johann, *A Picture of
    England* 72, 74–5
Defoe, Daniel:
    The Family Instructor 56
    Robinson Crusoe 16
Delafield, E.M., *Thank Heaven Fasting*
    177
delicacy (as sought-after quality in
    partner) 16–17, 28–9
Dell, Ethel M., *The Way of an Eagle*
    166–7
department stores 132
desperation, demonstrated by
    advertisers 48, 61–2, 98–9, 168,
    185
Devonshire, Georgiana, Duchess of
    29, 50
Dineley, Sir John 69–72, *70*
divorce 36, 49, 185, 194
Donaldson, Hannah 167–8
Dormer, Mary-Ann 153, 155
Dorset County Chronicle 116
Duncan, Leslie Fraser 141–4
Dunton, John 51

Edgeworth, Maria 51
    Belinda 29, 52
Edinburgh Courant 44–5
Edward VII, King 163
Empire, British 113, 130, 138–9, 166,
    178, 179
etiquette books 111
Evening Standard 185
Evening Star 182

exaggeration (in ads) 118–19
    see also lies and lying
Exchange and Mart 178
Exit (magazine) 187

fairs and festivals, as meeting places 4
fake ads 139, 140–41, 144, 146, 148,
        156, 163–4, 174
    see also scams and fraud
fantasy:
    romantic 56–7, 58, 98, 121, 137,
        166–7, 172, 183
    sexual 64, 73
Farquhar, George, *Love and a Bottle* 11
feminism 186, 188–9
Fenton, Gladys 154–5
Fielding, Henry, *Joseph Andrews* 16
first Lonely Hearts ad 1, 12
First World War 167–8, 172, 184
Fisher, Kitty 62
Fitzgerald, Gerald 167
flappers 173
flu epidemic (1918) 169
Flying Post (newspaper) 14
fortune-hunters 74–9
Foster, George 96, 97, 99
    *An Accurate Account of the Trial of
        William Corder* 95, 97, 106
France 87, 175
Fraser's Magazine 111–12, 119
fraud and scams 83, 144–56, 163–4,
        167–8, 178, 192
    see also breach-of-promise; fake ads
French Revolution 60, 79, 81
friendship and companionship ads
        161, 173–5, 180

Galignani's (newspaper) 87
Gardner, Sarah, *The Matrimonial
        Advertisement* 53–5, 79

gay ads 175–6, 186–7
    see also homosexuality
Gay Times 186
Gazetteer 62
gender ratios 131, 166, 168–9, 178, 183–4
General Advertiser 15, 20
Gentleman's Magazine 19, 29
George III, King 27, 32, 34
George IV, King (*earlier* Prince of
        Wales) vii, 83
Gloucestershire Chronicle 117
Gloucestershire Echo 153
gothic novels 59
Gregorina, Adelaide 88
Grimwood, Emma 151–3, 155
Guthrie, Sir Tyrone, *Matrimonial News*
        170–72

Haines, William 160
Hall, Frederick 153, 156
Hallberg de Broech, Baron von 118
Hardy, Thomas 104
Harrow School 122
health (as criterion for courtship)
        15–16, 191
Henrietta Maria of France 7–8
Hensey, Florence 17
Hibernian Telegraph 68
Highmore, Joseph, 'Mr B. finds
        Pamela writing' 65
Hoare, Prince, *Indiscretion* 65
Hogarth, William, *The Laughing
        Audience* 22
homosexuality 149, 166, 175–6, 180,
        186–7
Honeymoon (newspaper) 138
Houghton, John 2–4, 10, 11, 14, 40,
        166
Hunter, Kitty 56
Hunter, Maria, *Fitzroy* 64–5, 78, 79

ice rinks 138
India 111, 113, 130, 139, 179
Industrial Revolution 80, 114, 136
International Matrimonial Gazette 166
International Times 186
Internet dating 21, 128, 190–91, 193
Ipswich Journal 71
Isle of Wight 95, 101

Jackson, Frank and Edith 163–4
Jardine, Alexander 28
Jeffrey (magazine) 186
Jenner, Heather 184, 185–6
Jerrold, Douglas, *Wives by Advertisement*
   108–9
John Bull (magazine) 176
Johnson, Samuel 15, 34
joke and spoof ads 9–11, 19–20, 38,
   76–7, 82–3, 122–3, 153
Jordan, Alfred 149
Judd, Gertie (*later* Burnicle) 157–60,
   159, 180

Katherine Allen marriage bureau
   185
Knowles, Gladys 141–4, 155

Ladies Mercury 51
Lady's Magazine 18, 58
Lady's Monthly Museum 56
Landru, Henri-Désiré 175
Ledger (newspaper) 33
Leech, John, *Love in a Maze* 110
Leeds Intelligencer 119
Leeds Mercury 117, 119, 124, 131
Leman, Charles 150–51, 156
lesbian ads 186
libraries 65, 67
Licensing Act (1662) 3, 14
Liebert, John 126–7

lies and lying (in ads) 16, 40, 106,
   151, 153–4, 167–8, 174
   see also exaggeration; fake ads; joke
      and spoof ads
Link, The (magazine) 174–6
literacy 51, 136
Lloyds Weekly Newspaper 123, 152
Locke, John, *Two Treatises of Government*
   6–7
London:
   coffee-houses vii, 11, 17, 21, 24, 43,
      44, 65
   libraries 67
   population growth 7, 21–2, 114
   prostitution 79
   pubs and inns 1, 13, 44, 96, 123
   rise of the City 12
   shops 43–4, 65, 132
   theatres 21, 22, 23, 108
   urban loneliness 36, 114–15
London Chronicle 21
London Review of Books 193
'Lonely Soldier' ads 167
looks (as criterion for courtship) 2,
   14, 15, 20, 29–30, 35, 139, 182, 191, 193
love, and marriage 26–7, 30–32, 46,
   121, 166–7, 194
Lucan, Richard Bingham, 2nd Earl of
   87–8

Macfarren, George, *Winning a Husband*
   80–81
Mackenzie, Henry, *The Man of Feeling*
   57
Maclaren, Archibald, *The New Marriage
   Act* 86
Manchester Examiner 131
Manchester Times 143
marriage:
   arranged marriages 4, 26

average ages for marrying 2, 48,
    131, 193
eschewed by only one human
    society viii
joking about 9–11, 76–9, 80–82
love and 26–7, 30–32, 46, 121,
    166–7, 194
rates of 136, 178, 183, 187, 193
a social, economic and political
    necessity viii, 6–7, 26, 48–50,
    136–7, 164–5
see also common-law marriage;
    divorce
Marriage Advertiser 133
marriage agencies, brokers and
    bureaux 4, 83–7, 110, 139, 144,
    184–6, 190
Marriage Gazette 128
Marten, Maria 89, 91–6, 101–3
Mary II, Queen 6, 11
Matchmaker, The (newspaper) 168,
    176–7
Matrimonial Chronicle 138
Matrimonial Circle 166
Matrimonial Courier 138
Matrimonial Gazette 166, 178, 179
Matrimonial Herald 133–6, 139, 144–50,
    145
Matrimonial Intelligencer 138
Matrimonial Magazine 30, *31*, 74
Matrimonial Mascot 166
Matrimonial News 126, 127–8, 128–31,
    139, 140–41, 144
Matrimonial Post 137, 139, 140, 178,
    179–80, 182
Matrimonial Record 133
Matrimonial Register 138
Matrimonial Standard 166
Matrimonial Times 128, 138–9, 166,
    178–9, 182

Matrimonial World 138
Mercurius Fumigosus 8
Mercurius Matrimonialis 10
Mercurius Publicus 9
metaphors (used in ads) 122, 129
Milbanke, Annabella (*later* Baroness
    Byron) 87
Milne, Ada 126–7
Moncrieff, W.T., *Wanted: a wife* 81
money (as criterion for courtship)
    2, 14, 15, 17–19, 26, 30, 32–4, 119–
    20, 129–30, 182, 190, 191–2
    see also fortune-hunters
Morning Advertiser 71
Morning Chronicle 36, 82, 189
Morning Herald 82, 96, 97
Morning Post 73, 74, 82, 85, 143
music halls 137, 164, 172–3

Na people viii
New Statesman 182–3, 188, 189–90
News of the World 123
newspaper trade, growth of 14–15,
    20, 21–2, 72, 123–4, 128, 136, 140
Newton, Richard 78
Norfolk News 148
Norwich Mercury 28
novels, popularity and influence of
    16–17, 30, 51, 56–7, 59, 63–4, 166–7,
    183
Nussey, Henry 120

O'Connor, T.P. 139, 167
'Once Seen' ads 13–14, 20–23, 40,
    42
Oracle (newspaper) 178
Orwell, George 178–9
Otto, Charles 146–7, 149
Owen, Thomas 176–7

Pall Mall Gazette 131, 133, 137–8, 139

Pembroke, Henry Herbert, 10th Earl
    of 56

Phillips, Edward, *The Misteries of Love
    and Eloquence* 5

photography 139

Pimm, Beatrice (*later* Clarkson)
    169–70

Pitcher, William G. 148–9

Polstead, Suffolk 90–91

Poor Robin's Intelligence (journal) 9–10

Post Boy (newspaper) 14

Prager, Alfred 144

Prediction (newspaper) 178

pregnancy, out of wedlock 68, 99,
    136, 189

Private Eye (magazine) 181–2, 186–7,
    187–8, 189, 190

prostitution 49, 62, 79, 174

Public Advertiser 15, 61, 62, 67

pubs and inns 1, 13, 44, 123, 137,
    172

Punch (magazine) 124, 138, 169

Radford, Eleanor 182

railways 123

Reading Mercury 37

Red Barn murder case 90–106, 108,
    109, 112, 117

Reeves, Samuel 13

Restoration comedies 7, 11

Reynolds, Frederick, *Fortune's Fool* 79

Reynolds's Newspaper 123, 125, 155–6

Richardson, Samuel:
    Clarissa 16
    Pamela 16, 64
    Sir Charles Grandison 49

Riesman, David, *The Lonely Crowd* 35

romantic fantasy 56–7, 58, 98, 121,
    137, 166–7, 172, 183

romantic novels 56–7, 64, 137

Round-About (magazine) 161–3, 162,
    164, 173, 187

Rowlandson, Thomas 81, 84

satire 9–11, 19, 78, 81

scams and fraud 83, 144–56, 163–4,
    167–8, 178, 192

    see also breach-of-promise; fake
    ads

Second World War 178–9, 184

secrecy (about using ads) 3, 44, 80,
    157, 160

sex (mentioned in ads) 119, 176, 180,
    187–8

sexual fantasy 64, 73

sexual liberation 160–61, 179, 186–90,
    193

shared interests (as criteria for
    courtship) 122, 161

shopping 132

Shoreditch Observer 125

Skates, John Charles 146, 149

Smyth, William 175

Snagg, R., *The Newspaper Wedding* 59

social skills (as criteria for courtship)
    27–8, 34

Society for Checking the Abuses of
    Public Advertising 139

Southey, Robert 73, 80

Spanish-flu epidemic (1918) 169

Spare Rib (magazine) 186, 188–9

spinsterhood, fear of 131–2

Stamp Act (1712) 15

Stead, W.T. 161

stock markets 109, 128–9

Strand Magazine 173

Sun, The (newspaper) 139

Sunday Times 97

Surrell, Timothy 36–7

Sutton, Henry 149
swingers' ads 187

Tatler, The 13–14, 20
Tennyson, Alfred, 1st Baron, *In Memoriam* 163
theatres, as meeting places 21, 22, 23, 109, 137
Time Out (magazine) 187
Times, The:
    18th century ads vii–viii, 37–42, 47–8, 52–3, 54, 61, 71, 76, 77, 80
    19th century ads 90, 106, 107, 117
    20th century ads 175
    coverage of Red Barn murder 90, 92, 102, 103, 104, 105–6
    founding of 37–8
Town and Country (magazine) 85
T.P.'s Weekly 167
transvestites 188, 189
Tring, Hannah 150–51, 155
Tulle, Horace 151–3, 152
Tunbridge Wells 126

Universal Daily Register 37
urban loneliness 35–6, 114–16

Valentine's Day cards 135
Vanbrugh, Sir John, *The Provoked Wife* 11
Vanity Fair (magazine) 125
Victoria, Queen 121, 122

Wallis, John 40

Walter, John 37, 40, 44
Warren, Charles 116–17
Way Out (magazine) 187
websites *see* Internet dating
weekends, compilation of ads during 14
Weekly Times and Echo 148
white slave trade 177
Wilde, Oscar, trial of 149, 166
William III, King 6, 11
William IV, King 109
Windsor 69
wit and humour (used in ads) 37
    see also joke and spoof ads
Wollstonecraft, Mary 62
    Mary 63–4
    Thoughts on the Education of Daughters 50
    Vindication of the Rights of Women 28, 29, 57, 64
Woman's Weekly 183
women's magazines 51, 58, 183
women's rights 79, 160, 163, 164–5, 172, 178
Wood, Evans 154–5, 156
World's Great Marriage Association 144–9
Wortley Montagu, Lady Mary 19, 48

Y.M., *Some remarks on matrimonial advertisements* 109–111, 113, 185
youth (as criterion for courtship) 2, 14, 27, 55, 119, 182, 191